A Simple book of motivation and inspiration to all aspects of life.

You as the individual can use this book for guidance, motivation, business, life, inspiration, leadership, team skills, spiritually and to help with love for yourself and for other's.

Everyone needs some inspiration, and these quotes will give you the edge you need to create your own and others success. So read on and let this inspire you.

As you read this your thoughts will know this is a source of guidance, especially in times of recent need.

Most of the time a quotation can give us the inspiration we truly need in times of struggle and hardship.

Quotations can motivate us in times of tribulations, and others in time of tribulations.

Success is never final but along with that failure is never forever, it is however, the motivation that we choose that matters the most.

I made my mistakes and that in-turn made me. My life mistakes have become my greatest wisdom. Your mistakes can also be your greatest wisdom. Sometimes falling flat on your face is now, in fact your greatest victory. Do not be scared to live and make a mistake. Do not live, by not living at all. Live by trying and not being afraid of a mistake. Living is your own victory, your mistakes are your victory. Bottom is sometimes the place people learn where, how to rise. Let your bottom be the beginning of your victory. Do not stop trying. Do not stop living because you are afraid. Live, live a full life, use everything you know and have to live. You never know where you will end up this time next year, all because you took a step forward into living.

Living is on its own, a victory and that's something nobody can take away from you. If I die tomorrow, I know I have lived, I am not ready to die of course I want to live more, but I know I could rest easy, knowing what life really is. Do not let a day pass by, without living each day at your best, even if this said day, you do not perform your best or you made a mistake, guess what you lived it still. What a great relief to each night before you sleep, that you have lived this day to its full potential.

Go on, go and enjoy living, enjoy learning, enjoy adjusting your sail on your path, enjoy learning who you really are without media or anybody else telling you who to be. Your life, is your creation. Do not stop learning what you love, what you enjoy, who you really are. Once you know yourself, learn more if you want to, perfect the subject which is you, constantly work on perfecting who you really are.

Title, I have to many titles that I would like to name this short book. However, this is just a few that had crossed my mind:

Guidance is the key to humanity.

What our souls desire.

The universe is more than just skin.

Love is hope and hope is love.

Guidance costs nothing.

You are a free spirit, do not be trapped.

Your smile can make the world shine.

Love is free.

Encouragement is just a few words.

Life is love.

Peace can for eternity.

We all have each other's back.

Kindness is the new cool.

You may decide this book should be renamed to something different, that is your right. This book is to represent we have our own minds and we have a free will to use it, without being judged.

So go ahead and rename this to your heart's desire.

Contents

Acknowledgements.

Introduction

Quotes

Summaries

Acknowledgements

There are many who have inspired me in my life. Many who have given me encouragement and been an outstanding example of how human beings should behave, even in times of hardship.

I am humbled at times by the kindness and generosity of the human species and this inspires me.

I have been inspired to continue the kindness, I have inspired to give even when I have nothing. Yes, my own hardship has taught me many lessons, although, lessons and hurt, I have taken the greater good from those lessons. I took away the greater good, because of those around me, whom truly shown an outstanding character of strength, and shown that by given there upmost they do encourage others to be lifted back into strength and positivity.

There are so many individuals I would like to thank for inspiring me to become a better human being, however it would be impossible for me to name all of these individuals, I do not know personally all of those people who have gave me inspiration, but their actions in the world have inspired me. The following, are the people I know personally that have inspired me, I would be remiss not to mention the following:

Help 4 homeless veterans. (David, Tom, Jean, Steve)
Myself.
Brandon Casey.
Johnny Leyland Randoll Guymer.
Melissa Wilson.
Jodie Gibson.
Zoe Louise Lannin.
Jade Gallagher.
Gemma
Andy Gearing.
Kelly Marie Younger.
Pippa

It is vital that we all remain at least a little enthusiastic when facing any venture, or we can only expect more of the same. Life is not an easy task, but you shall not remain in your defeat, and when your defeat gets you down you are only prolonging your success. Make an effort with yourself and those around you to remain with enthusiasm, especially regarding future endeavours, regardless of how many times you have fallen in your past, or even now in your present. When momentum of enthusiasm and motivation is built, this enables you to easily feel excited and determined about your next venture.

Introduction

Inspiration, kindness and motivation can go a long way.

A quote a day may possibly change the day you have.

All you have to do, is believe.

We can all change this world one day at a time. There is no problem with the colour of people's skin, there is no problem with the height or weight of somebody, there is no problem with your strengths and weaknesses, there is no problem with somebody's personnel beliefs.

Why do certain people make these problems?

Exactly, I do not know either. Does media and society make us believe we have to be prejudice? Is it a friend or foe who makes us believe we have to judge others in certain ways?

I cannot answer exactly why equality and diversity is a problem, but I can tell you this…

We as the human race, we are all equal. It does not matter if my beliefs are different to yours, or if my skin colour is different to yours. We all have bones and muscles with a layer of skin. We all have a heart made out of a muscle. We are all some kind of chemical or cell put together. So why the need for us all to be prejudice?

Why don't we, as the human race stick together and change our future.

We after all are the same species. We all live on this planet, we all eat and breathe of this planet.

We have no idea when the human species may be extinct. So we should all put our heads together and make our life wonderful.

We are all souls inside a skin.

We all deep down just want love and happiness. We are all sick of being hurt, scared, frightened and judged.

Why don't we stop judging each other and start loving each other? Let's not ignore or provoke attacks on our differences and start embracing them.

Okay, so you may be rich and famous, but how are you any different to the homeless man?

Well, the difference is you were maybe born into another path, you had a different journey or you worked hard (not saying this homeless person has not) or you knew how too, because you had the knowledge.

But, how are you different? The answer is, you are not. Your luck could leave you at any point, you have had different struggles, but still found life tough as well as easy, you got lucky and your path led you to where you are now, you have still probably made just any many wrong choices as the homeless individual, however it may have affected you in another way.

I am not judging you by the way, I think it is amazing you are in the position you are in life, you certainly are an inspiration to many including myself, but the point I am trying to say is; Just because the homeless man has had a bad streak of luck, does not mean he/she does not have a degree, has not worked hard, had luck in their lives.

It means each type of human being on this earth will always be at different levels to each other.

How boring would the world be, if we were all rich, famous and not facing challenges.

How would you grow as an individual if everybody's' path was exactly the same and easy? Okay, well I may contradict myself now.

Life is hard and everybody is on a different path, why do we all need to struggle to the point of suicide and illnesses due to stress, lack of nutrition and lack of hygiene. We don't need to struggle to this degree. Yes, struggle is a path of life.

Your finding yourself.

Your learning your interests and dislikes.

Your learning your skills and attributes.

However,

I say this with passion.

Shall we as a world, as a nation, as a city, as a town, as a neighbour, as a friend or foe start helping each other, even if it is with just your truly beautiful smile.

Knowledge. Do not be selfish with knowledge, if you know something share it with the person next to you, then they share it. Spread knowledge not gossip, but knowledge that will help and guide others.

Love. Do not be selfish with love, if you have love, share it. Share it with everybody. Make every person you meet smile. Show them there is love in this world. Show them how amazing they and you are. Show another person that your soul is beautiful, however do not forget to remind them just how beautiful they are also. None of us know exactly how long we have on this earth (no matter what your beliefs) we are only in the human skin for a certain time period, so be remembered. Be remembered for being kind, leave a good impression, help those around you.

I guarantee your heart will feel less strained and more at peace, just by helping another person. You will have a sense of pride, like never before. You will make yourself smile. You in-turn will be a better person and be remembered as a kind, loving human being.

Food. Do not be selfish with food. Us human beings do not need everything we eat to survive. Our bodies can perform highly, on a particular amount of calories. However, there are some human beings who are not getting even half of that, homelessness and starving worldwide. So why are we eating more calories than our body needs? Why is there a rise in obesity in this world, along with a rise of starvation in other parts of the world? Why, because we are greedy, we do not need all this food we intake.

The world is running out of food as I write this and before I wrote this, it is only going to get worse. Why don't we share our food with the starving, let's all be equal? Because the reality is, we become obese and some humans will starve and die, our future generations are going to run out of food and then the last of the human race will starve to death (yes, this is the worst case scenario and I'm taking maybe hundreds of years). Why don't we preserve now, eat what we need, share what we need so all can survive? Of course have some luxury's every now and then, enjoy yourself, its living, but don't die obese whilst the homeless man starved to death. If we have a sandwich, give half to the homeless man, the starving child.

Share.

I can honestly say from the bottom of my heart, that peace and love really can make this world a better place.

Although, I cannot do it alone, I will need all of your help to ensure peace and love is implanted. Overall love can sometimes win. Shall we as a nation, as a world turn sometimes in to every time.

I believe, excepting each other's flaws and giving guidance to perform better in life, will make this world a better place.

I believe, we can still lift up another human being, even with our last strength and change their lives.

I believe, loneliness can in the end kill somebody or at least drive them to insanity. Try not to leave anybody alone. Do not let others feel lonely. Let everybody feel part of something.

I believe, bullying is wrong and in the end, it's a cycle. You get bullied, so you bully someone, that persons end up bullying someone and so forth. The Cycle has begun.

Why don't we stop bullying? Cut that cycle, don't encourage abuse to each other. After all, we are all only human. We do make mistakes and that is okay. We do not perform perfect all the time, we are human. We do not look outstanding every day, we may sometimes have a skin break out, our hair not setting exactly how we want it to. We are only human.

We do not all look the same, but why do we judge those who look extremely different to ourselves? I can't tell you why we judge.

I think we judge, because we are all deep down scared of the unknown, which is by the way, normal. Its normal to be wary of the unknown. We are human. This is a natural instinct of any species. When something different arrives we get a sense of being intrigued. Just like a pack of animals, just like them we will try and understand something different, until we know we are safe. Although, unlike animals, us humans like to attack the unknown. Animals usually only attack if they feel fear or if their lives are actually in danger. But us humans we can be evil, we attack someone with a disability, with different skin colour and beliefs, but why? We are not in danger. This is not a risk to our lives. We can be a seriously horrible species at times.

We do not need to attack another human being who looks or believes or even behaves differently to us. We need to love and guide and support. That's what we should do as human beings.

Unfortunately, we have learned behaviour going back thousands of years to attack whatever is different to us. We of course are top of the food chain, well that is in earth anyway. Who knows what else is in the world. But because we are top of the food chain, because we have achieved more than somebody else, because we are bigger than others, because we are richer than others, it does not give us the right to attack one another, it does not give us the right to say nasty words and to physically hurt somebody. We are all equals. We should all help and guide each other. We all only have one life as a human being. We all should put aside our differences and start respecting each other opinions. No I am not saying agree with what everybody says, because that would take away our individuality, but I am saying we should respect and listen to others opinions. We should not attack somebody for being different. We of course are all allowed our own opinions. For e.g.

I hate these shoes, so I won't purchase them or wear them, but you are wearing the shoes I hate, should I shout abuse at you, or physically hurt you. No, no I should not and I would not. I for one; have no right to treat you like that. Two; are you attacking me with your shoes, is my life in danger, because your wearing these shoes? No. Three; it is what you like, I respect that and they probably look amazing on you, even if they didn't on me, you obviously think they do. So why would I go out of my way to hurt your feelings, over something that is not a threat to me. That's your style, your likes and I respect that.

We should all act in this way.

We have so many individuals all over the world that are an inspiration to us all. We have so many individuals all over the world that help others without being recognised. They help others in their own accord and from the kindness in their heart, they deserve recognition. However, these particular individuals are not acting in kindness for recognition, they simply are doing this for the greater good of the human race and for love and kindness. These individuals cannot stand to see others hurting in any way shape or form.

We have those in power who are in a great position to help and aid others, these individuals inspire myself along with many others to act in such a manner of kindness, support, respect and love.

We as a species can help all these individuals, the ones in power or the ones who act in silence, we have the strength as a world to aid and help with each cause. We also have the power to lift another human being without being rich. All we need to do is show kindness and kindness cost nothing. Kindness is a smile, a hug, sharing you sandwich and taking your time to talk to somebody. You perform these small acts of kindness, you may possibly change somebody's day, somebody's outlook on life, somebody's life. When this individual is feeling stronger, they will remember what you did for them that day, you may have been a stranger, but the cycle of love and kindness has just begun. This person will never forget how you made them smile and they will do the same for the next person, they may see who needs some kindness.

We have many cycles in life, although it is down to us what cycle we choose. Do we as a nation, world choose the cycle of abuse or should we choose the cycle of love.

I personally, am going to choose the cycle of love. We can all stop this cycle of abuse together. It may take years; it may take months. It takes courage to truly show kindness and love especially when you feel personally depleted.

We as humans have courage and strength built within us. I believe in you all. We all have love. We all have a smile. We all have inner strength and we all have a heart.

Let you love shine, let hope be the new light, let peace be our new storm.

When you are hurting, I will take your hand gently and I will listen. I will show you I care and I hope you would do the same for me.

Make our new world peaceful.

The following pages; will consist of Motivational, Inspirational, love and Kindness poignant quotations to inspire you for the following days and forever more.

When you feel depleted, take a look at the required quotation and pick yourself up, smile and soak in your surroundings and carry on with your quotation in mind.

Of course, not all quotes have been written personally. Although I believe you will find these useful in the future and forever more.

Please smile and believe in yourself, believe in those around you and this beautiful world, do not let anybody make you sad, make you feel disappointed in yourself, life is hard enough without others degrading us, you fight back with kindness and strength, encourage all the kindness you have and turn this world around to what we know it can be.

If you personally struggle with people around you, whom are negative or are volatile, please read the quotations to encourage and lift you for guidance and strength.

If you adore a good quotation or poignant phrase look towards the quotations for fun and strength and perhaps create your own too.

Don't be afraid, as they say; no question is a stupid question, effort made, is the start of reaching your full potential, however we have to start someone.

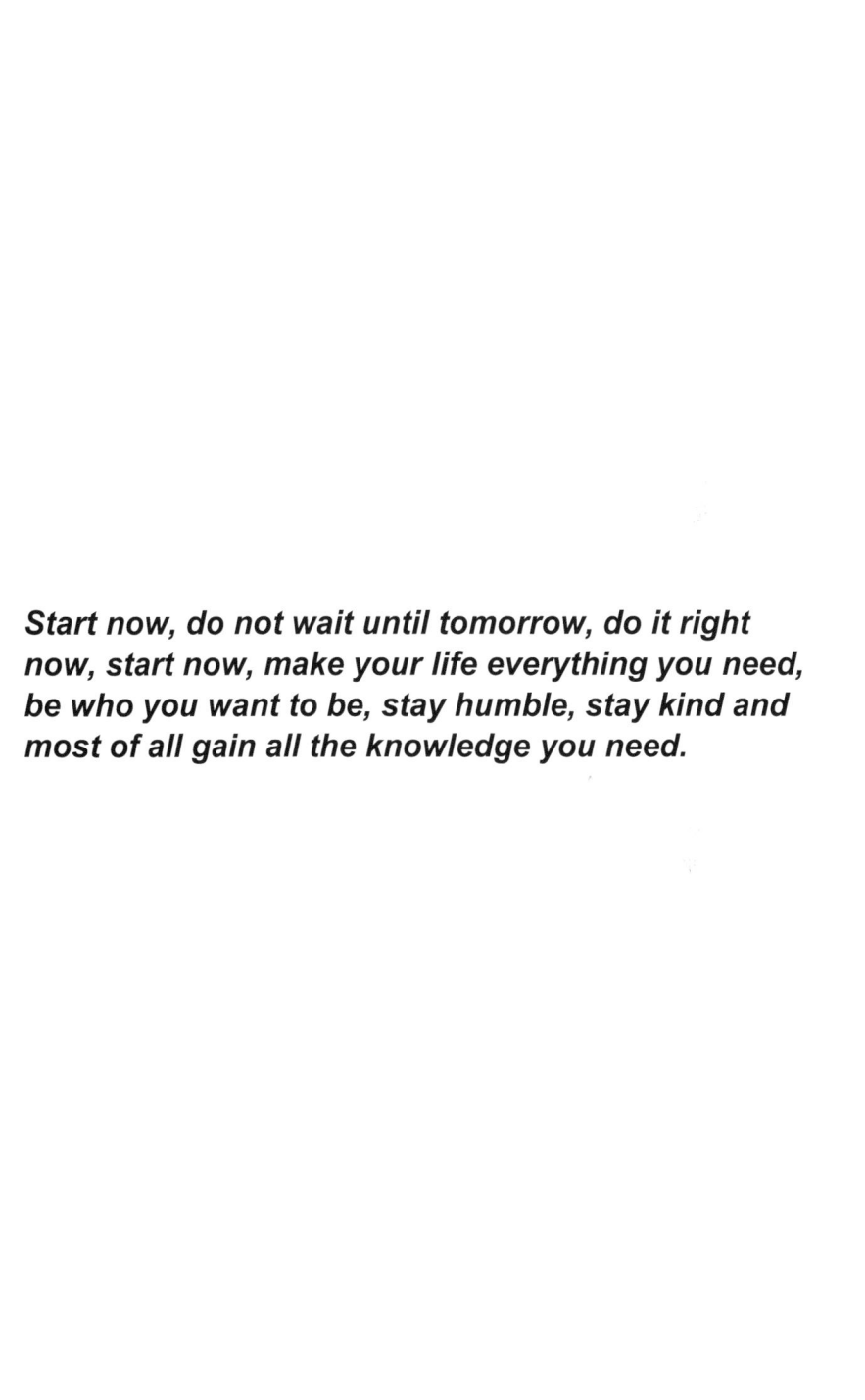

Start now, do not wait until tomorrow, do it right now, start now, make your life everything you need, be who you want to be, stay humble, stay kind and most of all gain all the knowledge you need.

Quotations and Poignant phrases

'You are the dreamer of your dream'

'healing light'

'always with you'

'my happiness is a direct reflection of my level of faith in the universe'

'all is divine'

'all is seen and known'

'joy is the ultimate creator'

'play full innocence'

'the moment I realign with love; clear direction is presented to me'

'rising phoenix'

'light is magical'

'the presence of love will always cast out fear'

'hearts wisdom'

'natures love'

'I choose to learn through love'

'natures beauty'

'forest whispers'

'my fearless freedom lights up the world'

'listen with care'

'I let go of the shadow of the past, by seeing someone for the first time with the eyes of love'

'dive deeper into you'

'instead of praying for an outcome, I pray for the highest good for all'

'transformation'

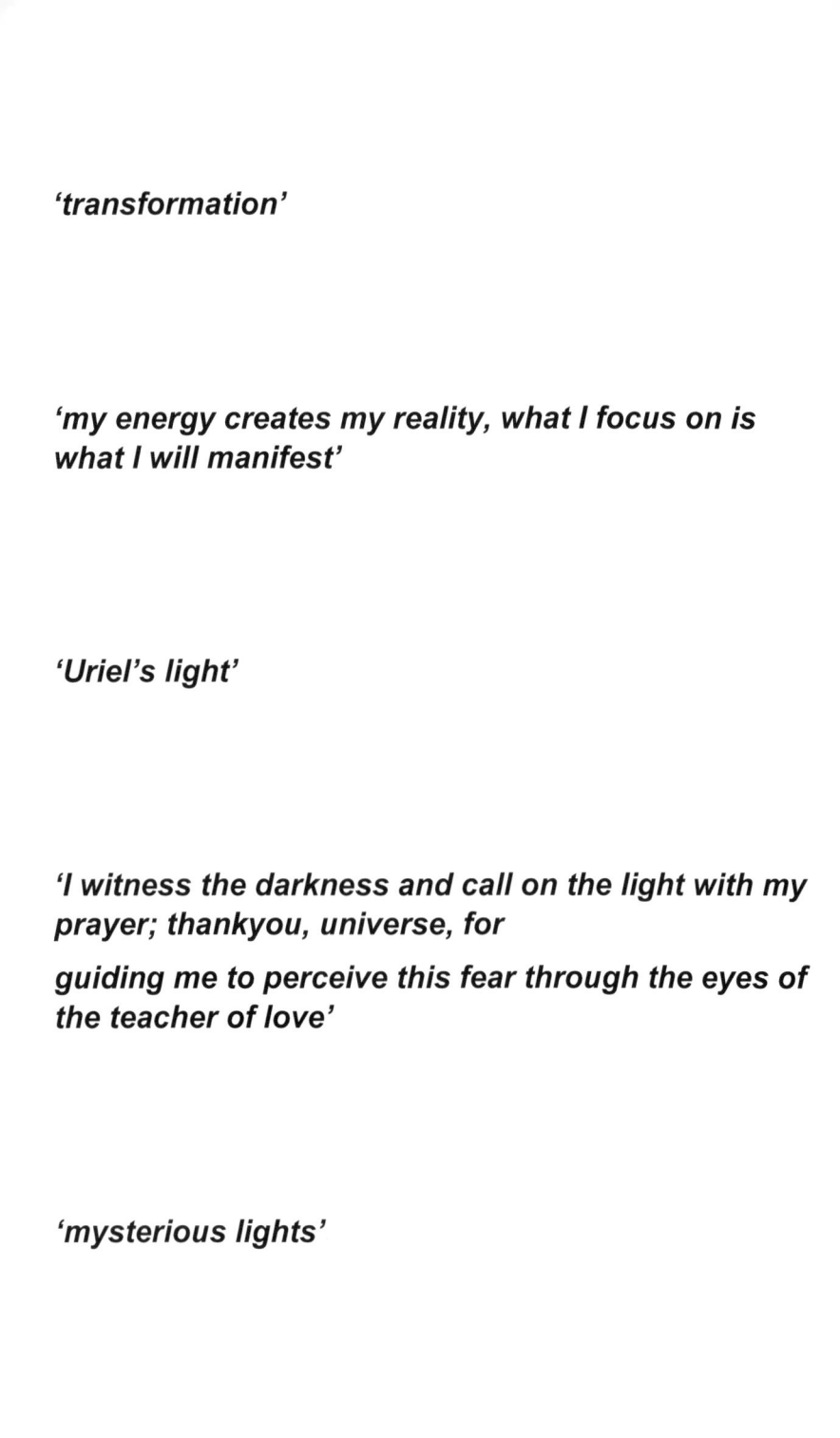

'my energy creates my reality, what I focus on is what I will manifest'

'Uriel's light'

'I witness the darkness and call on the light with my prayer; thankyou, universe, for

guiding me to perceive this fear through the eyes of the teacher of love'

'mysterious lights'

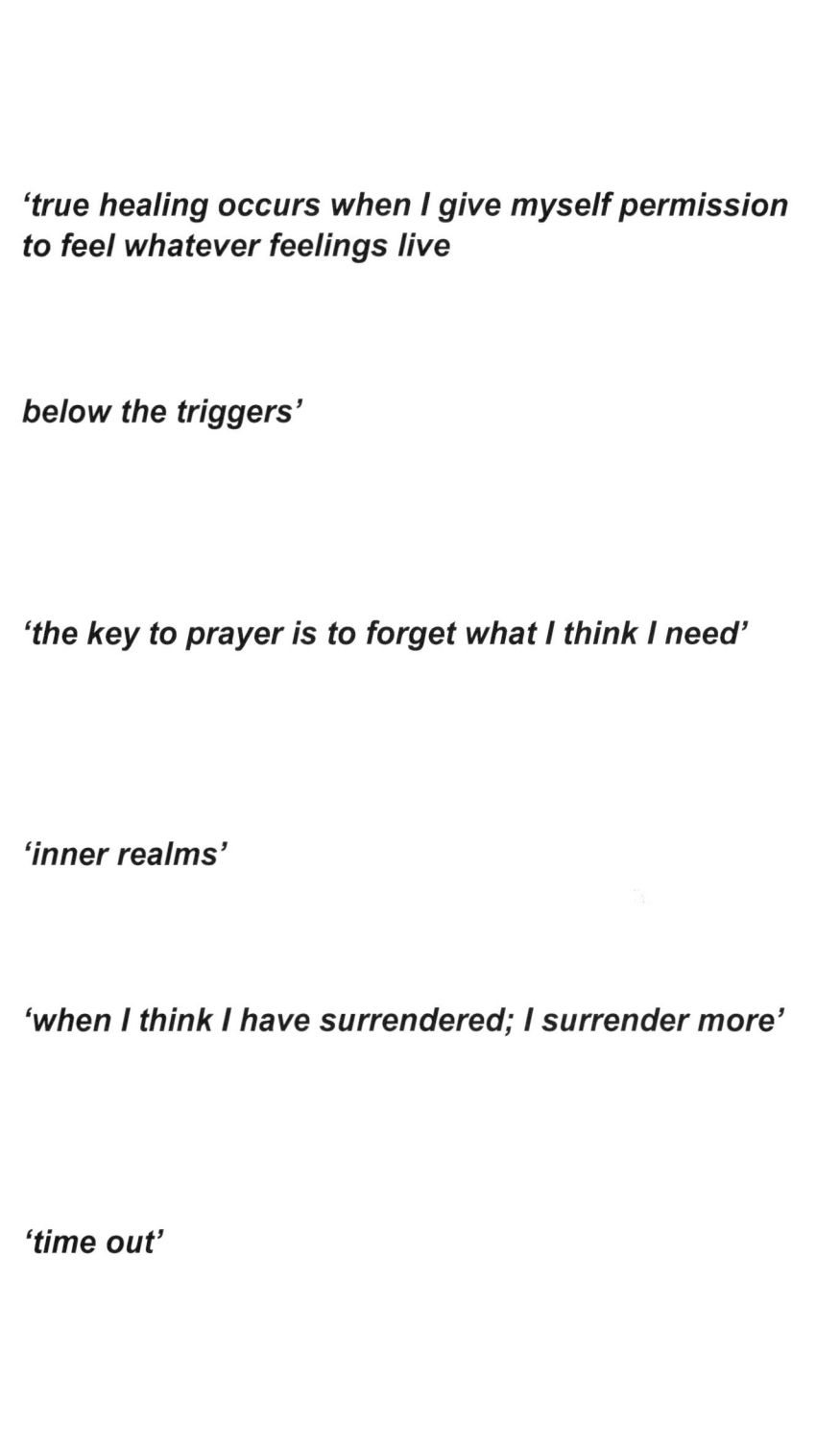

'true healing occurs when I give myself permission to feel whatever feelings live

below the triggers'

'the key to prayer is to forget what I think I need'

'inner realms'

'when I think I have surrendered; I surrender more'

'time out'

'hidden spirits'

'when I lean on certainty and faith, I change my mind about the world I see'

'inner realms of light'

'movement creates lasting growth'

'I surrender to a power greater than me'

'holding you'

'hope is not lost'

'step forward'

'oneness is my true nature'

'there is a stream of love supporting my dreams'

''sword of truth'

'when I focus on my inner light, I see the world through the lens of love'

'take flight'

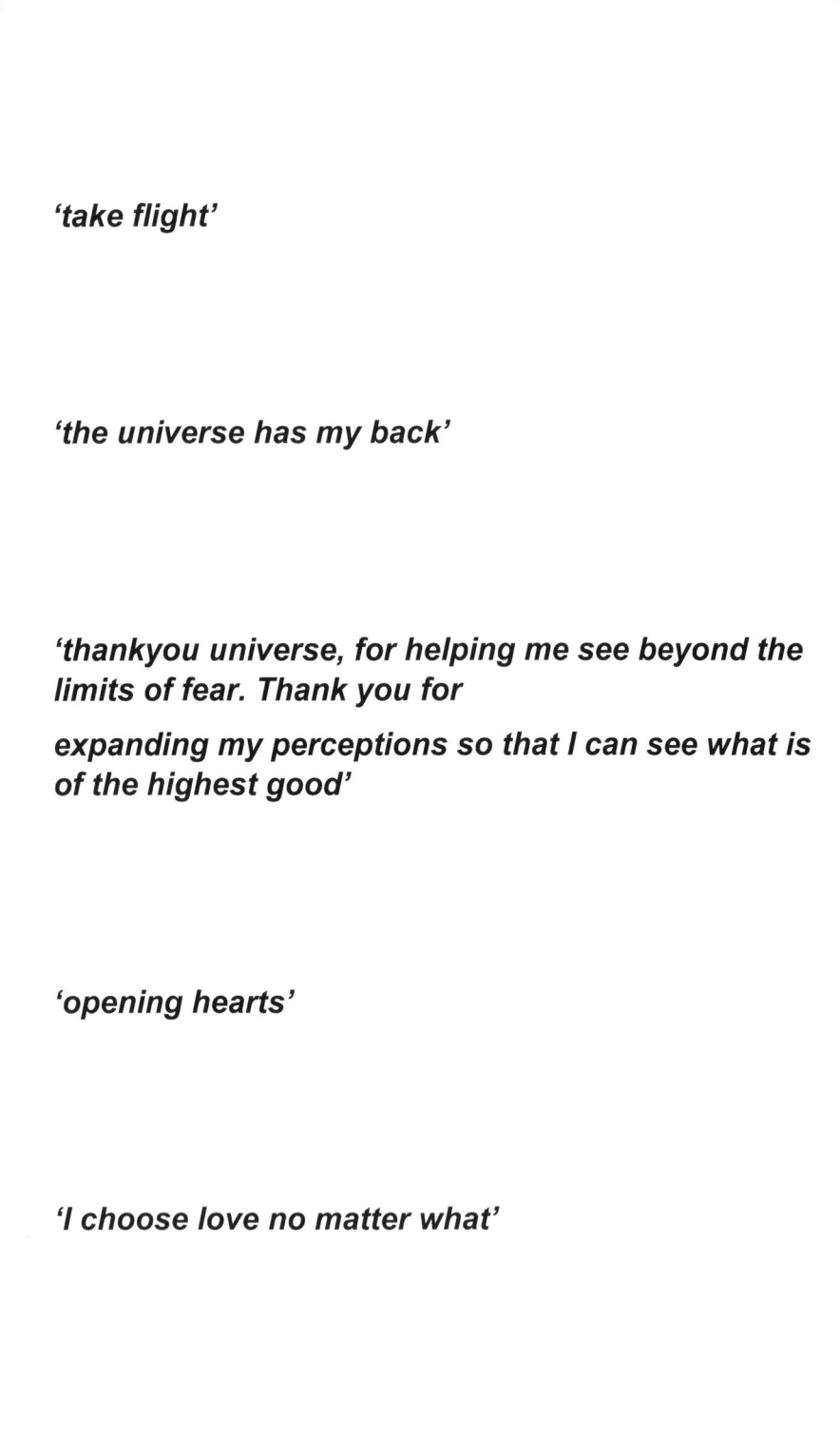

'the universe has my back'

'thankyou universe, for helping me see beyond the limits of fear. Thank you for

expanding my perceptions so that I can see what is of the highest good'

'opening hearts'

'I choose love no matter what'

'I am the dreamer of my dream'

'in any moment I can surrender to the powerful presence of love through prayer,

contemplation and stillness'

'fire fly creates change'

'peace is yours'

'energy flows where my intention goes'

'be willing to open'

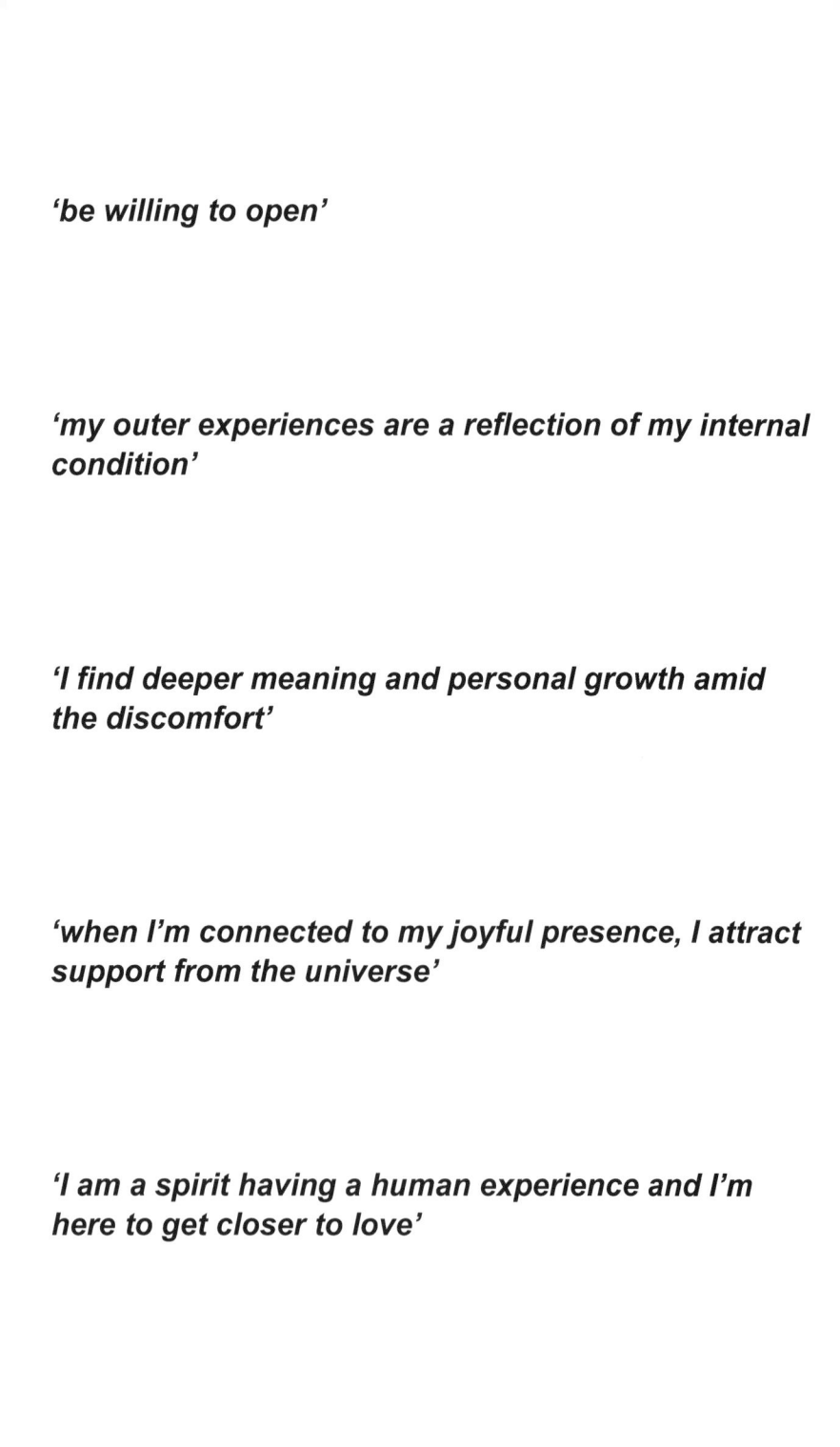

'my outer experiences are a reflection of my internal condition'

'I find deeper meaning and personal growth amid the discomfort'

'when I'm connected to my joyful presence, I attract support from the universe'

'I am a spirit having a human experience and I'm here to get closer to love'

'believe in yourself'

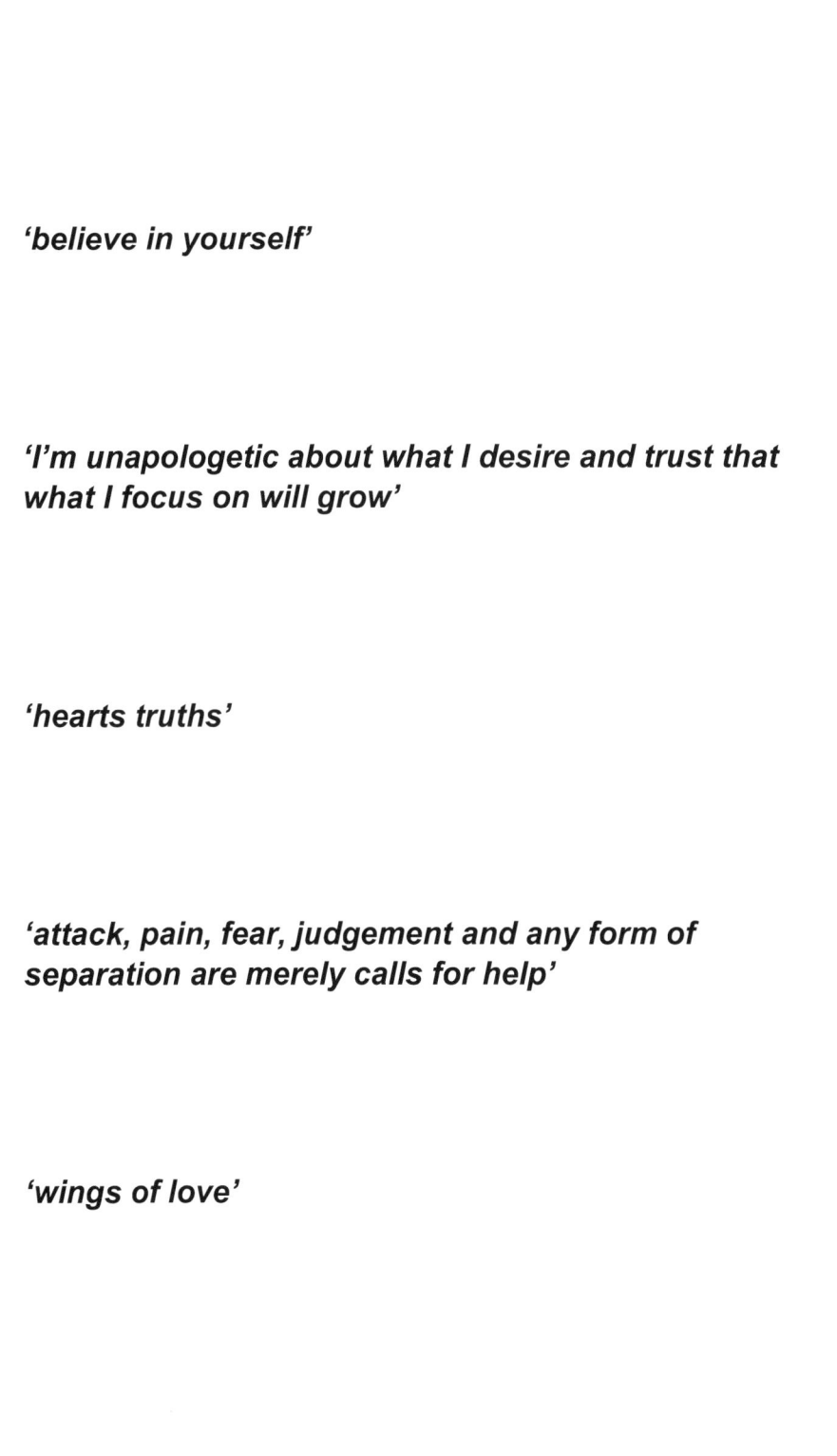

'I'm unapologetic about what I desire and trust that what I focus on will grow'

'hearts truths'

'attack, pain, fear, judgement and any form of separation are merely calls for help'

'wings of love'

'I honour how I want to feel'

'in every moment the universe is conspiring to bring me toward right-minded thinking

and the energy of love'

'natures secrets'

'the more energy and intention I bring to my faith, the more fearless and free I am'

'obstacles are detours in the right direction'

'when I accept the love of the universe as my primary teacher, I will always be guided back to the light'

'golden gates'

'the universe works fast when I'm having fun'

'I always trust the direction of the universe and know I'm being guided'

'I recognise that I have chosen fear, and I choose again, I choose love'

'there is nothing sexier than my authentic truth'

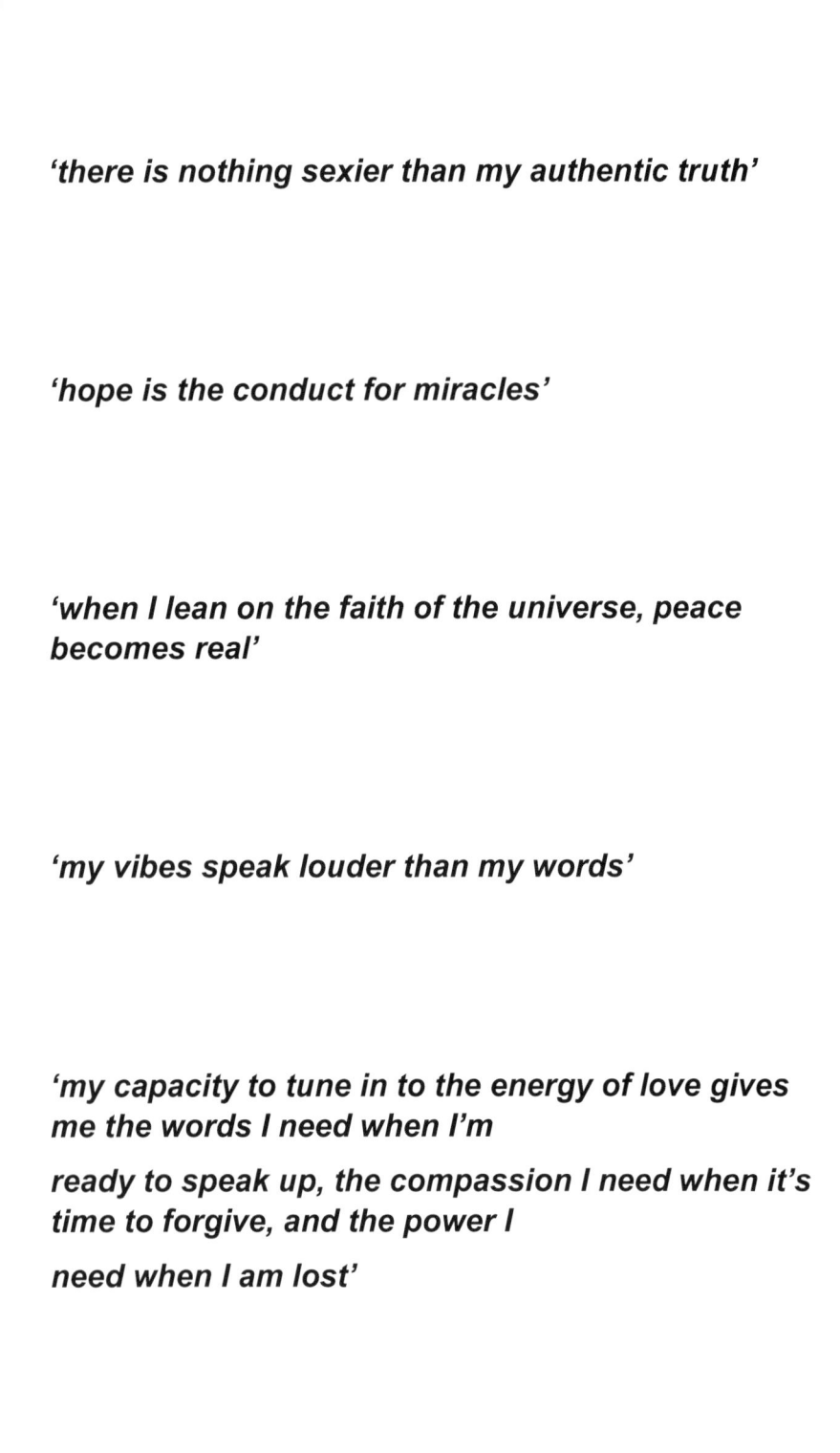

'hope is the conduct for miracles'

'when I lean on the faith of the universe, peace becomes real'

'my vibes speak louder than my words'

'my capacity to tune in to the energy of love gives me the words I need when I'm ready to speak up, the compassion I need when it's time to forgive, and the power I need when I am lost'

'daisy love'

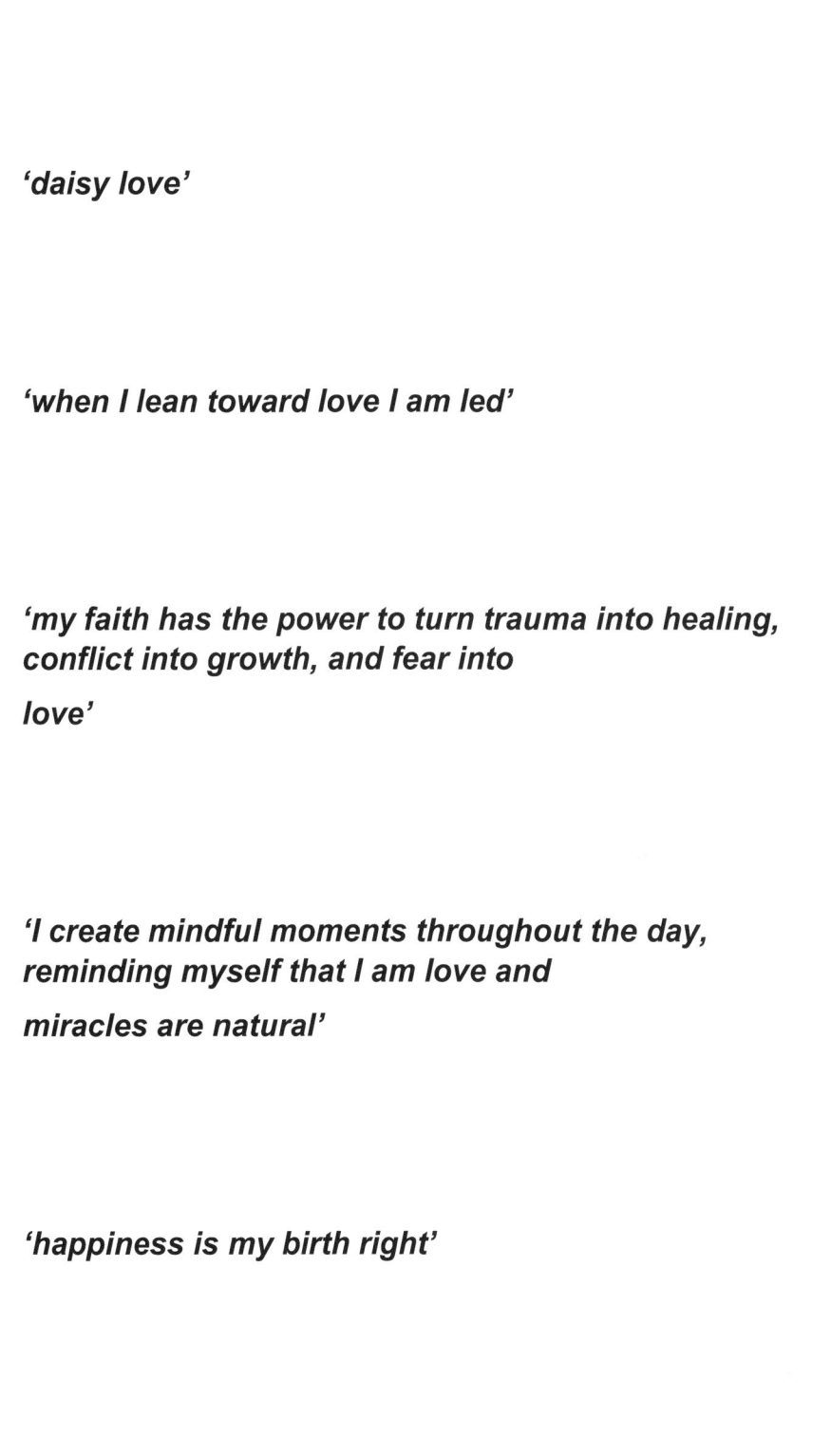

'when I lean toward love I am led'

'my faith has the power to turn trauma into healing, conflict into growth, and fear into love'

'I create mindful moments throughout the day, reminding myself that I am love and miracles are natural'

'happiness is my birth right'

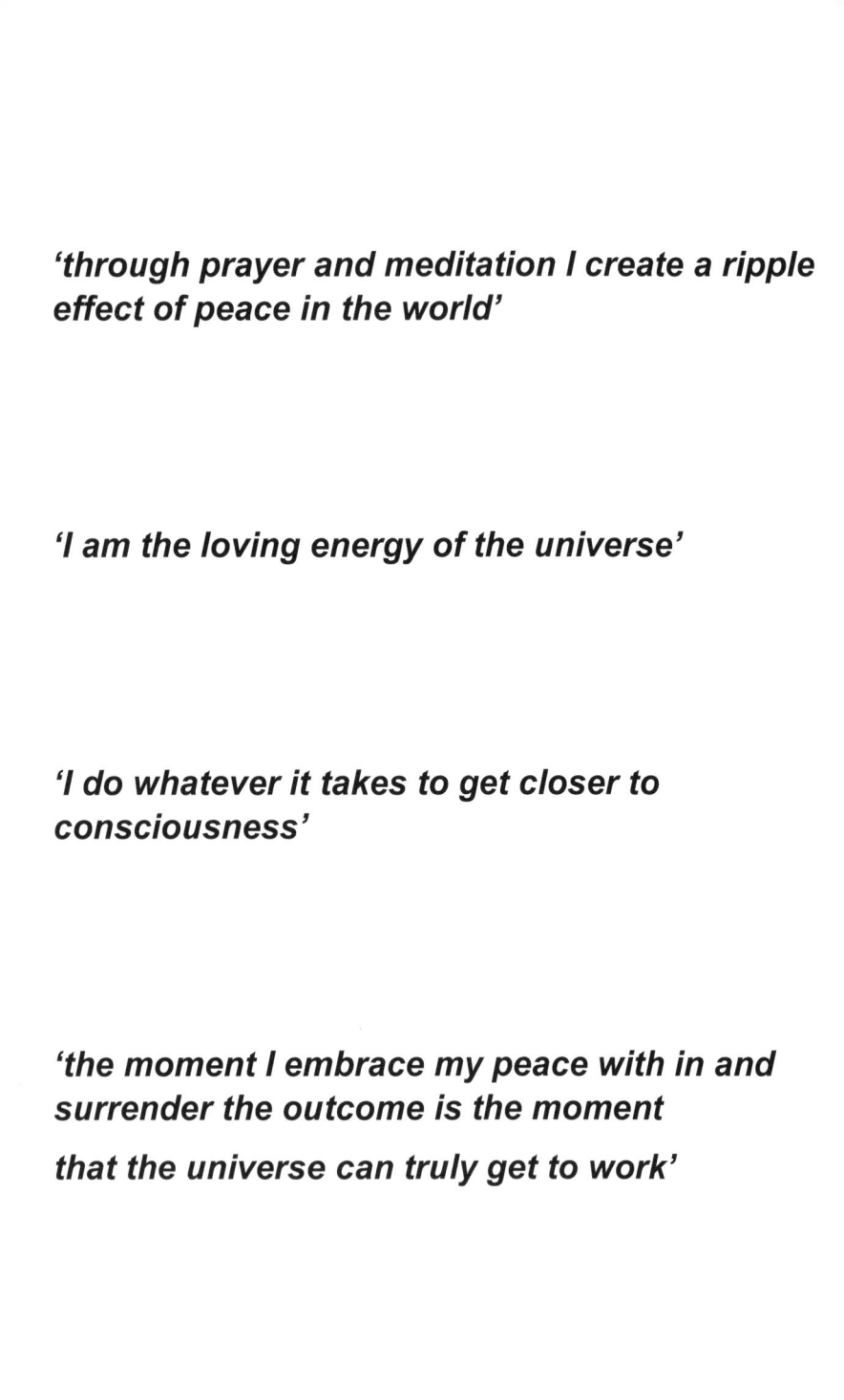

'through prayer and meditation I create a ripple effect of peace in the world'

'I am the loving energy of the universe'

'I do whatever it takes to get closer to consciousness'

'the moment I embrace my peace with in and surrender the outcome is the moment

that the universe can truly get to work'

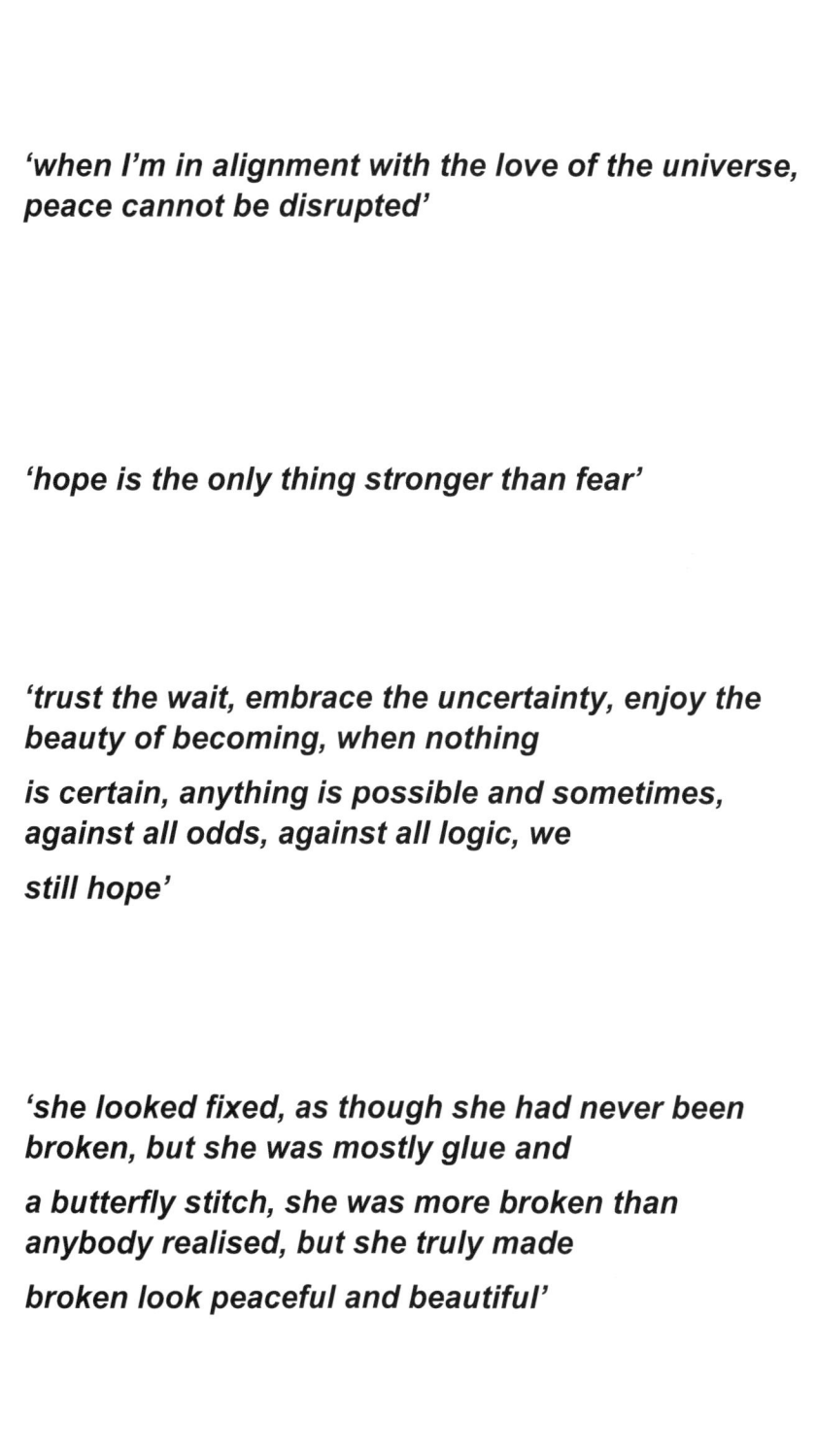

'when I'm in alignment with the love of the universe, peace cannot be disrupted'

'hope is the only thing stronger than fear'

'trust the wait, embrace the uncertainty, enjoy the beauty of becoming, when nothing

is certain, anything is possible and sometimes, against all odds, against all logic, we

still hope'

'she looked fixed, as though she had never been broken, but she was mostly glue and

a butterfly stitch, she was more broken than anybody realised, but she truly made

broken look peaceful and beautiful'

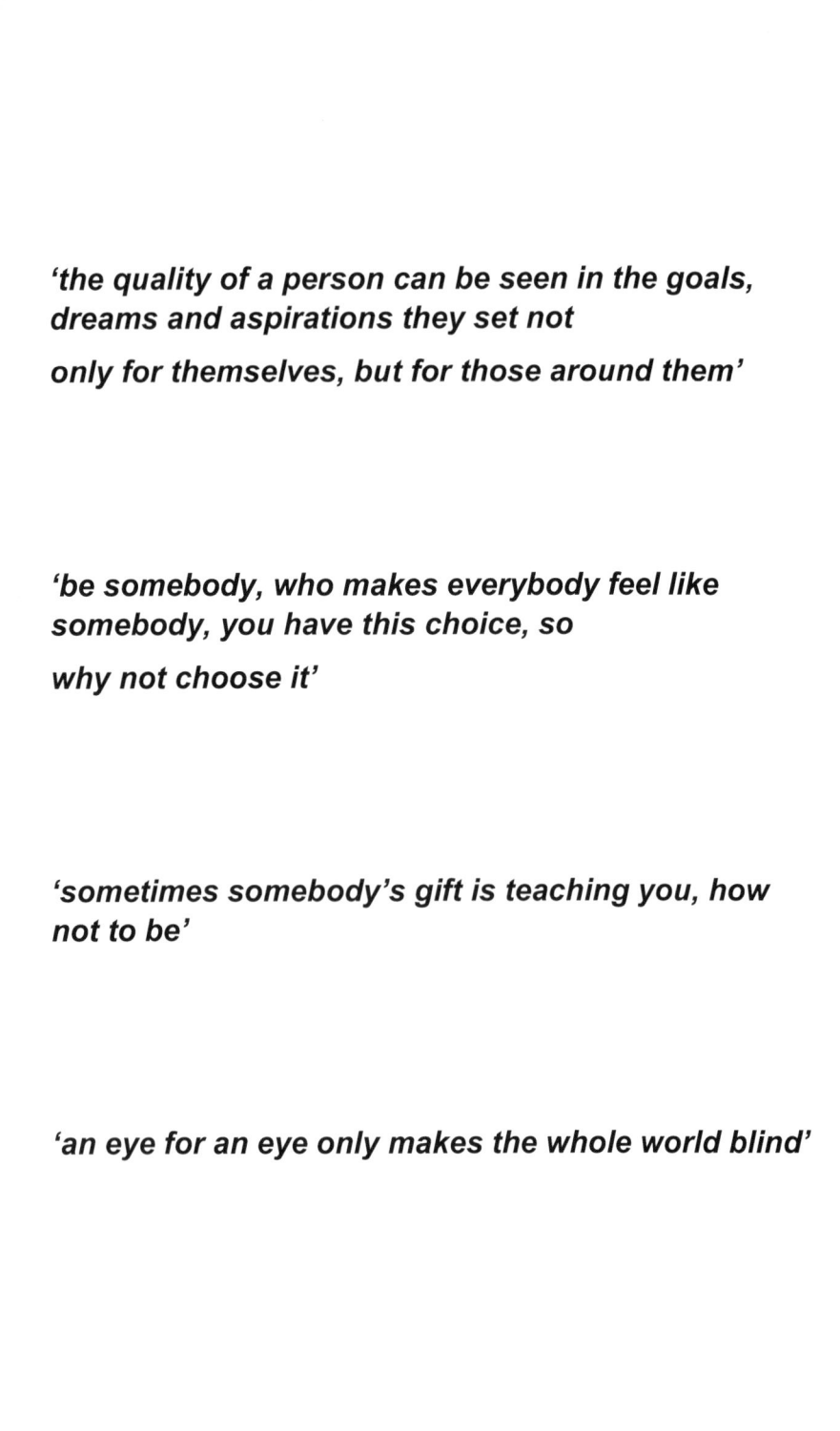

'the quality of a person can be seen in the goals, dreams and aspirations they set not

only for themselves, but for those around them'

'be somebody, who makes everybody feel like somebody, you have this choice, so

why not choose it'

'sometimes somebody's gift is teaching you, how not to be'

'an eye for an eye only makes the whole world blind'

'no matter how old anybody is, sometimes a person just needs a hug'

'I should hate you for all you have done to me. I wouldn't wish that pain on anybody.

You go around living life as if you have done no wrong, but the truth is you can be

selfish. All you ever cared about were your feelings, your wants and needs, me a

human being, I was just a porn in your games of lies. And even though I know I will

never get the apology I deserve, I forgive you because I owe it to myself to heal and I

owe it to myself to move on'

'it only takes a few seconds for us to hurt somebody, but sometimes it takes years to

repair the damage, take a few seconds to be kind instead'

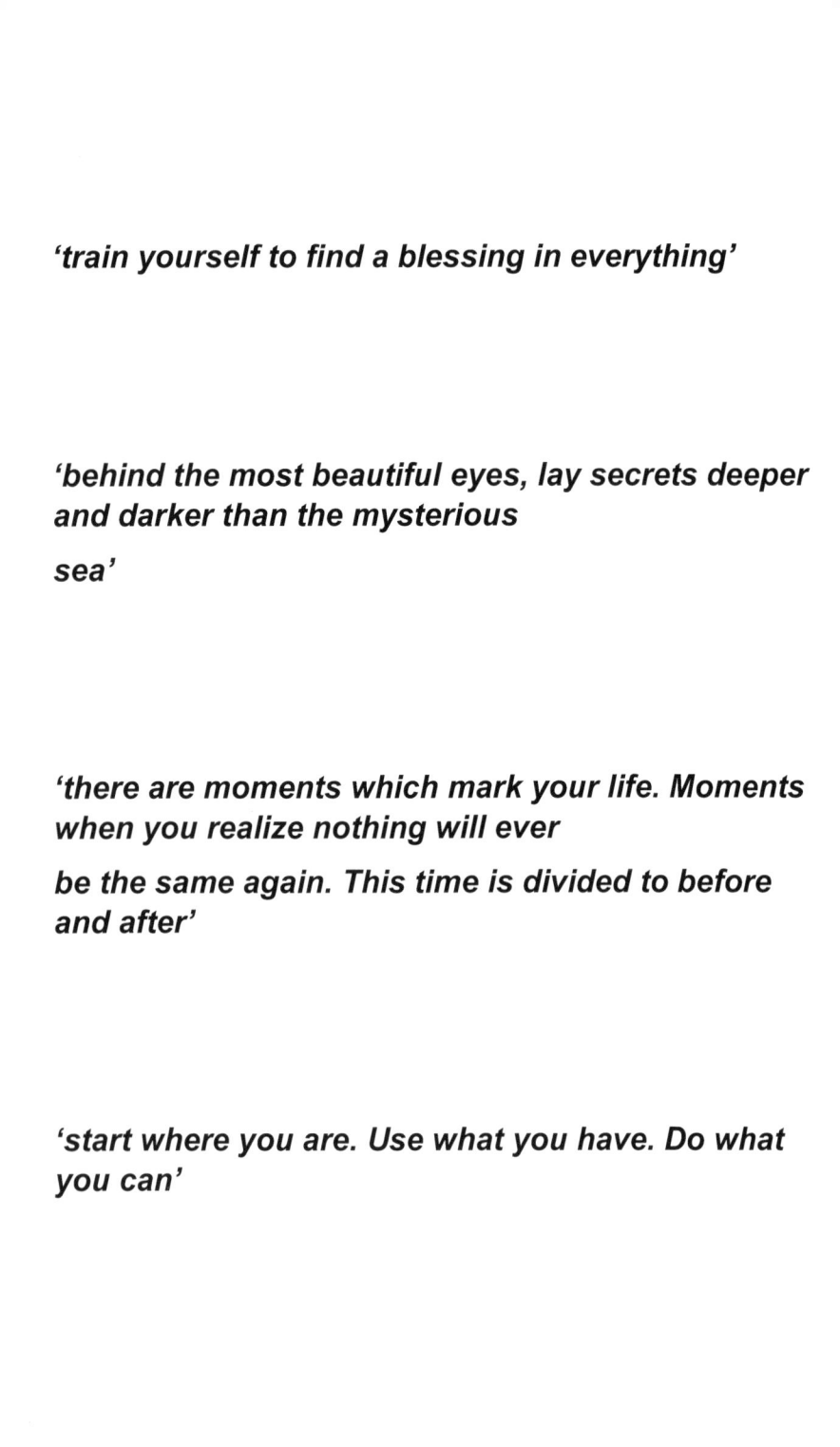

'train yourself to find a blessing in everything'

'behind the most beautiful eyes, lay secrets deeper and darker than the mysterious sea'

'there are moments which mark your life. Moments when you realize nothing will ever be the same again. This time is divided to before and after'

'start where you are. Use what you have. Do what you can'

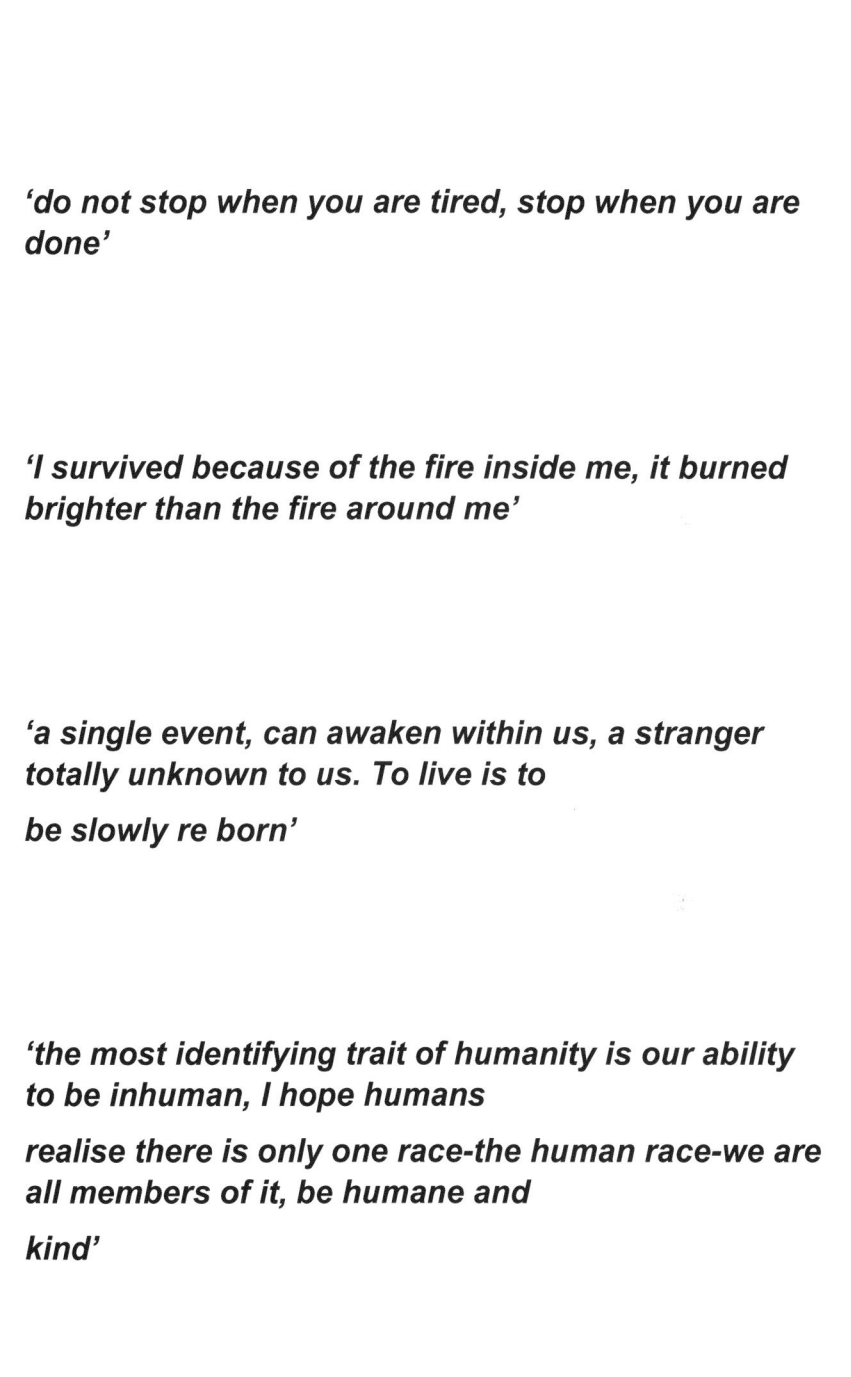

'do not stop when you are tired, stop when you are done'

'I survived because of the fire inside me, it burned brighter than the fire around me'

'a single event, can awaken within us, a stranger totally unknown to us. To live is to

be slowly re born'

'the most identifying trait of humanity is our ability to be inhuman, I hope humans

realise there is only one race-the human race-we are all members of it, be humane and

kind'

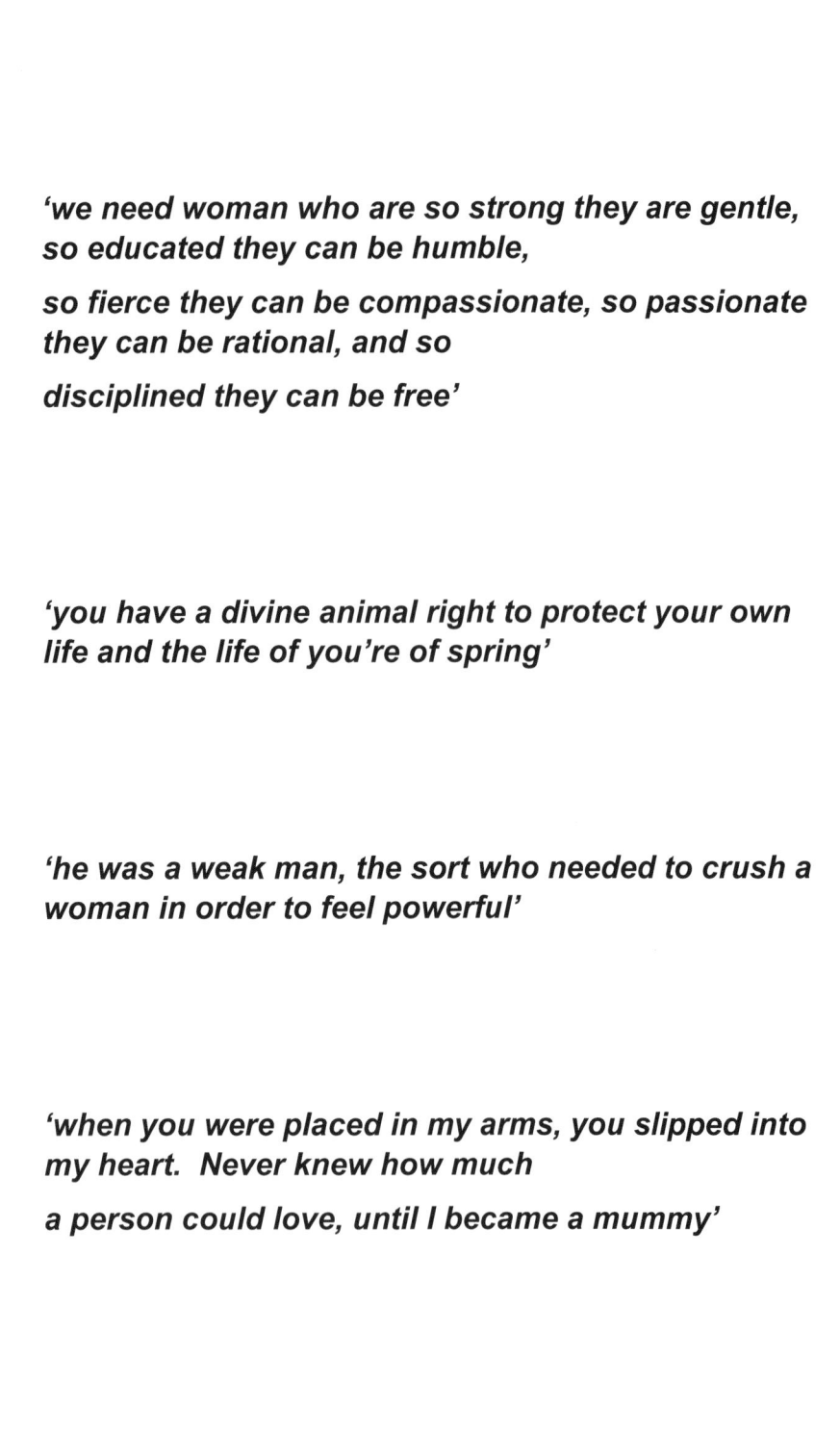

'we need woman who are so strong they are gentle, so educated they can be humble,

so fierce they can be compassionate, so passionate they can be rational, and so

disciplined they can be free'

'you have a divine animal right to protect your own life and the life of you're of spring'

'he was a weak man, the sort who needed to crush a woman in order to feel powerful'

'when you were placed in my arms, you slipped into my heart. Never knew how much

a person could love, until I became a mummy'

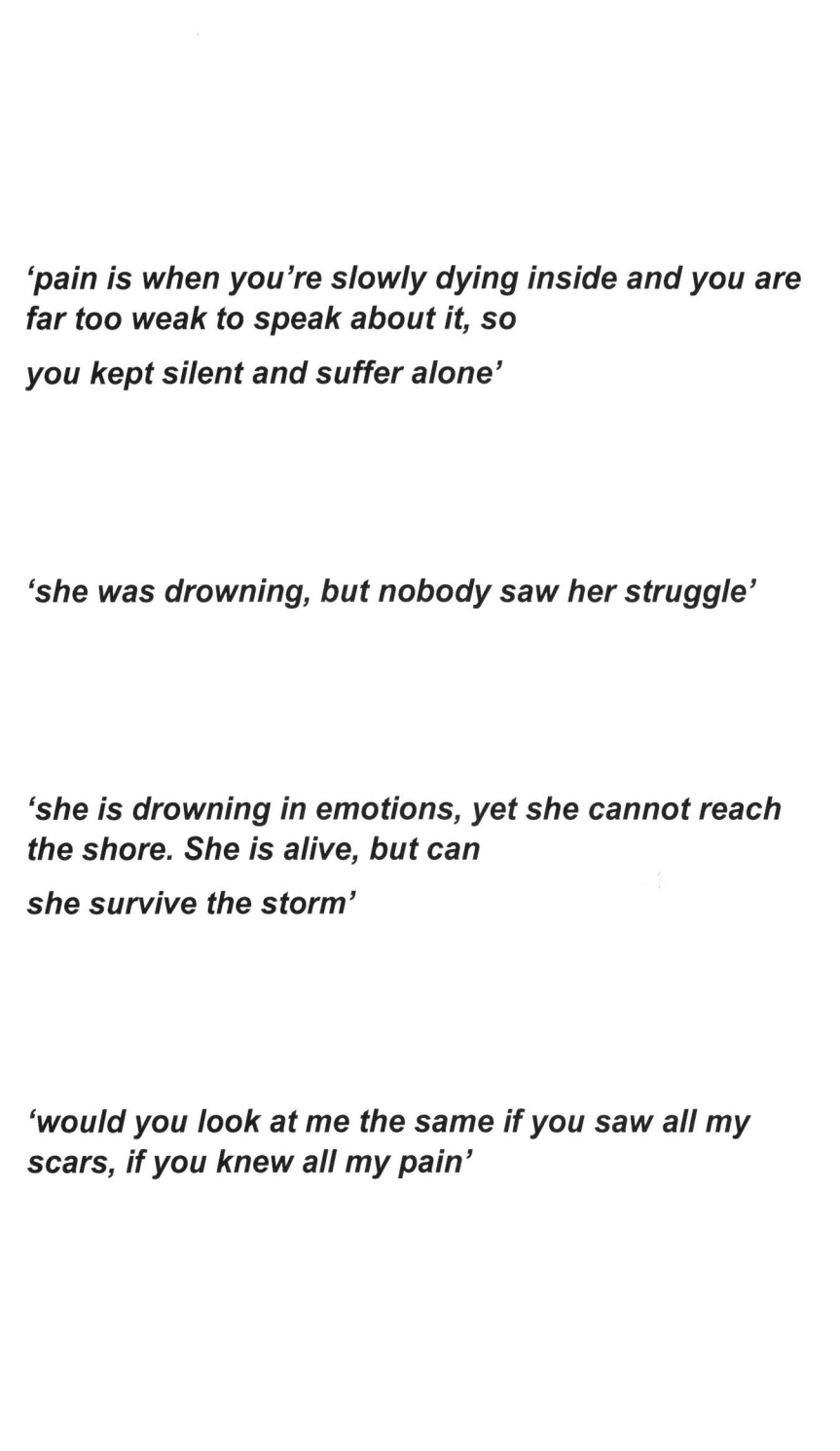

'pain is when you're slowly dying inside and you are far too weak to speak about it, so

you kept silent and suffer alone'

'she was drowning, but nobody saw her struggle'

'she is drowning in emotions, yet she cannot reach the shore. She is alive, but can

she survive the storm'

'would you look at me the same if you saw all my scars, if you knew all my pain' *'if you had not noticed, the scars on my heart or the fake smile on my lips along with*

the forced laugh I have adopted, the way I do not care about the things I used to love,

the true sadness hidden in my eyes, then do not dare stand at my grave and cry. How

can you cry for somebody you do not even know'?

'she is the type of girl who will hold you while you cry and stay up all night just to

make sure that you're okay, even if she is the one breaking sometimes'

'the spark in my soul grew back, the fighter, that part of me came back alive'

'my story can maybe change at least one person's life for the better'

'everything happens for a reason, with that said, it makes me a believer'

'my own flesh and blood, is my secret miracle'

'life is beautiful and if you think it is ugly, change your view'

'my job on this earth, is not yet complete'

'I still have more love and kindness to share'

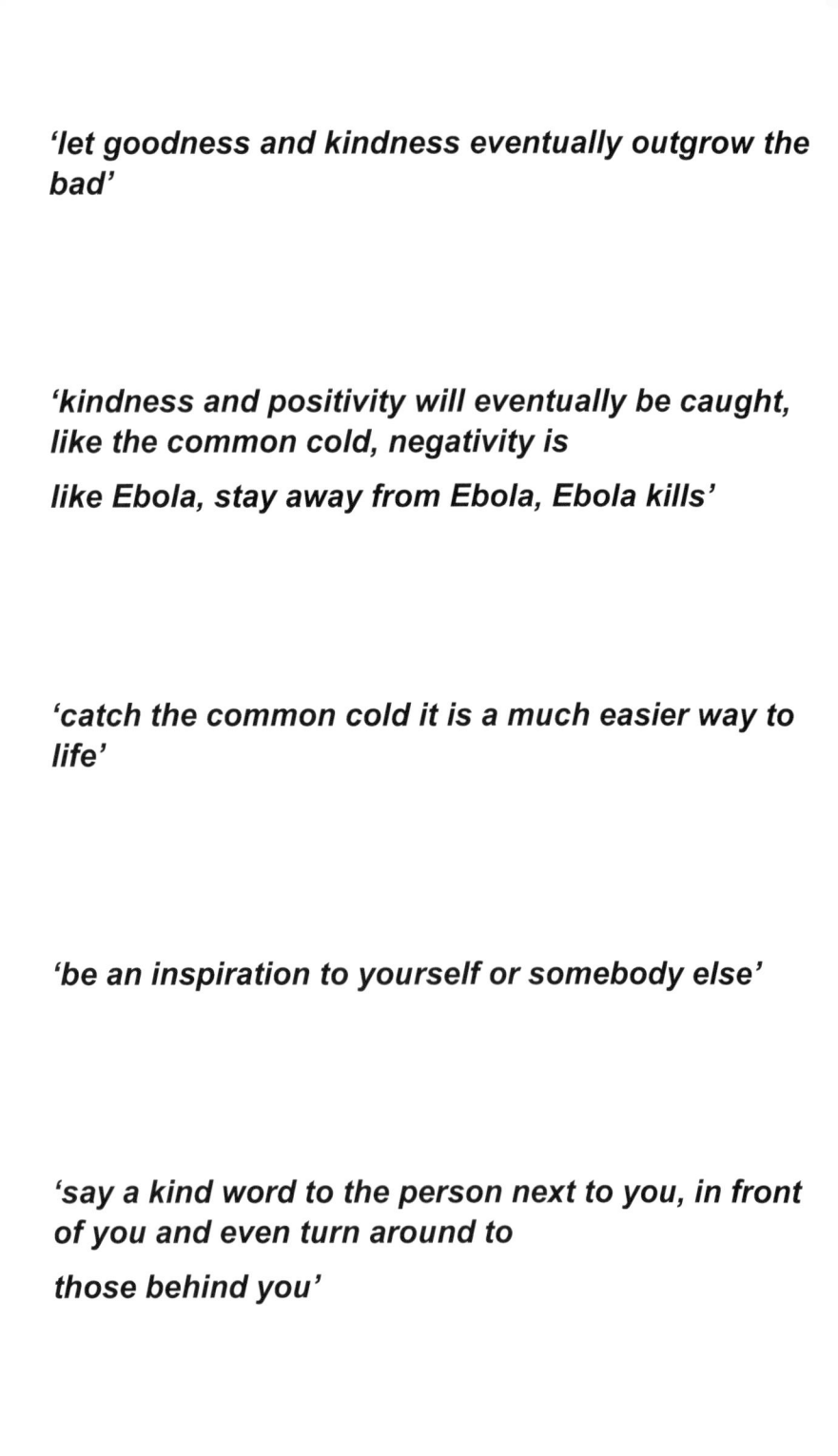

'let goodness and kindness eventually outgrow the bad'

'kindness and positivity will eventually be caught, like the common cold, negativity is

like Ebola, stay away from Ebola, Ebola kills'

'catch the common cold it is a much easier way to life'

'be an inspiration to yourself or somebody else'

'say a kind word to the person next to you, in front of you and even turn around to

those behind you'

'help one person a day, one act of kindness per day'

'make kindness the new cool, the new fashion statement, the new in thing, kindness is catchy'

'tell your stories if you want, you never know it may just inspire someone'

'record every thought that flourishes through your mind'

'have a goal and achieve it, make yourself proud'

'be humble and kind'

'be proud of how far you have come'

'have courage to achieve your aims'

'love yourself today'

'you do not need to compete with anybody around you, compete with your own

yesterday'

'everyone is in their own race in life, focus on yours'

'trees grow in silence, but a tree falls down with the loudest of noises'

'a flower does not compete with the flower next to them, it merely focuses on

themselves making them as beautiful as they can be, but let's not forget the flower is

not selfish, it does not trap a bee inside its petals, it lets the bee fly around freely,

using the pollen and transferring pollen to another plant'

'you have the power to keep going, even when you're in darkness, darkness is not

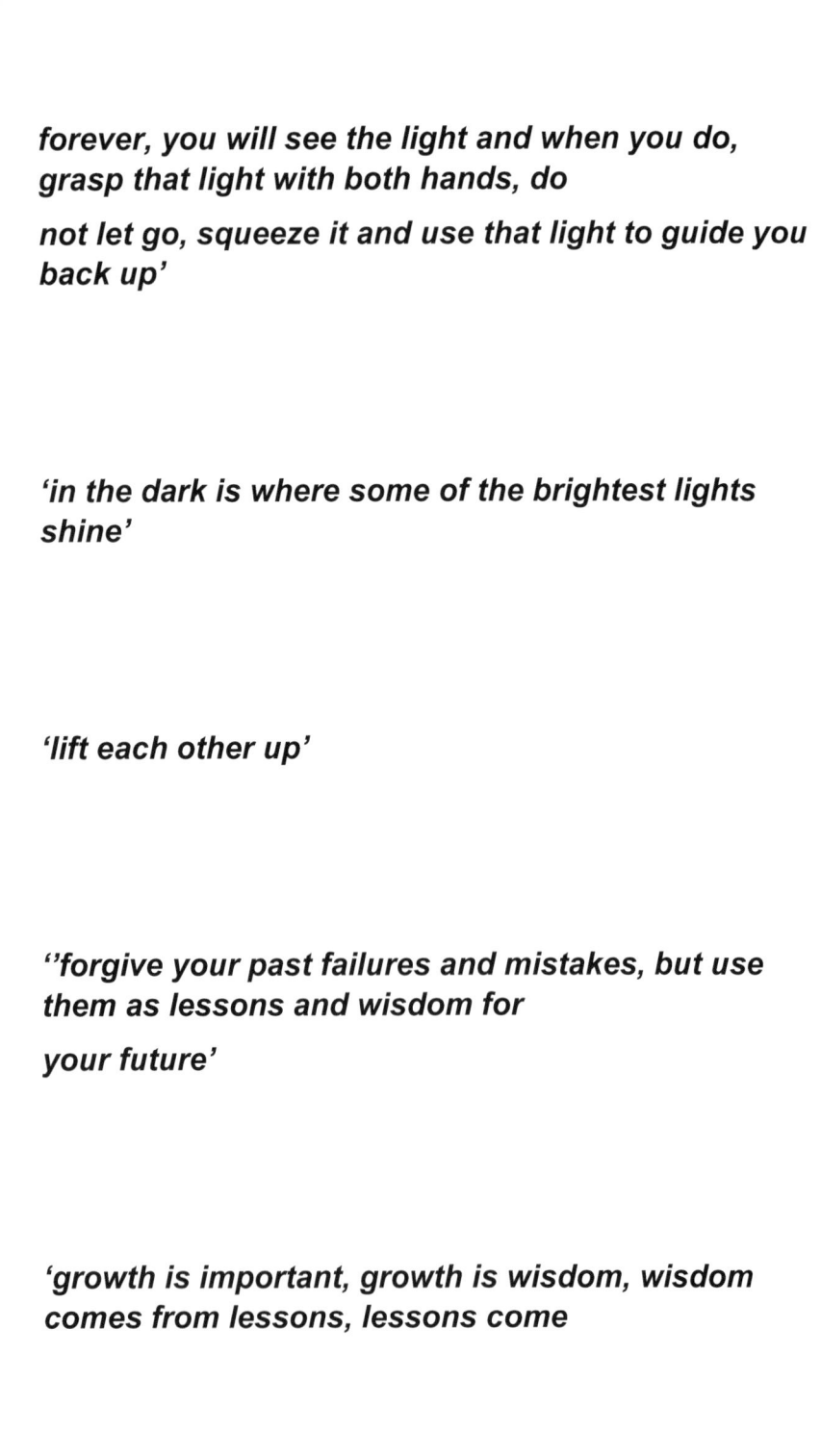

forever, you will see the light and when you do, grasp that light with both hands, do

not let go, squeeze it and use that light to guide you back up'

'in the dark is where some of the brightest lights shine'

'lift each other up'

''forgive your past failures and mistakes, but use them as lessons and wisdom for

your future'

'growth is important, growth is wisdom, wisdom comes from lessons, lessons come

from past'

'I believe in the power of kindness and support and strength and what it can do to this world'

'I believe in the power of positivity'

'smile as soon as you awake'

'smiles are catchy'

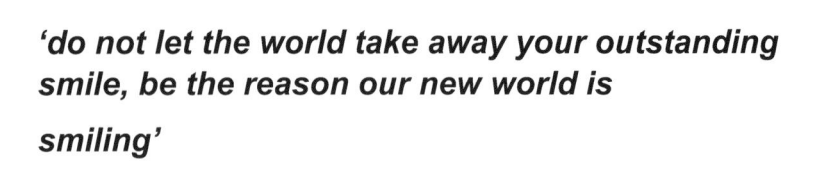

'do not let the world take away your outstanding smile, be the reason our new world is smiling'

'it is okay to hope; it is okay to survive. Life is surviving, but try and find the easiest survival you can and when it is tough, you hope like your life depends on it. Do not give up hope.

Inspirational humans from our past and present, our favourite quotes of theirs.

'if a friend of mine gave a feast, and did not invite me to it, I should not mind a bit. But

if a friend of mine had a sorrow and refused to allow me to share it, I should feel it

most bitterly. If he shut the doors of the house of mourning against me, I would move

back again and again and beg to be admitted so that I might share in what I was

entitled to share. If he thought me unworthy, unfit to weep with him, I should feel it as

the most poignant humiliation.'-- Oscar Wilde.

'A friend is someone who knows all about you, and loves you just the same'--Elbert

Hubbard.

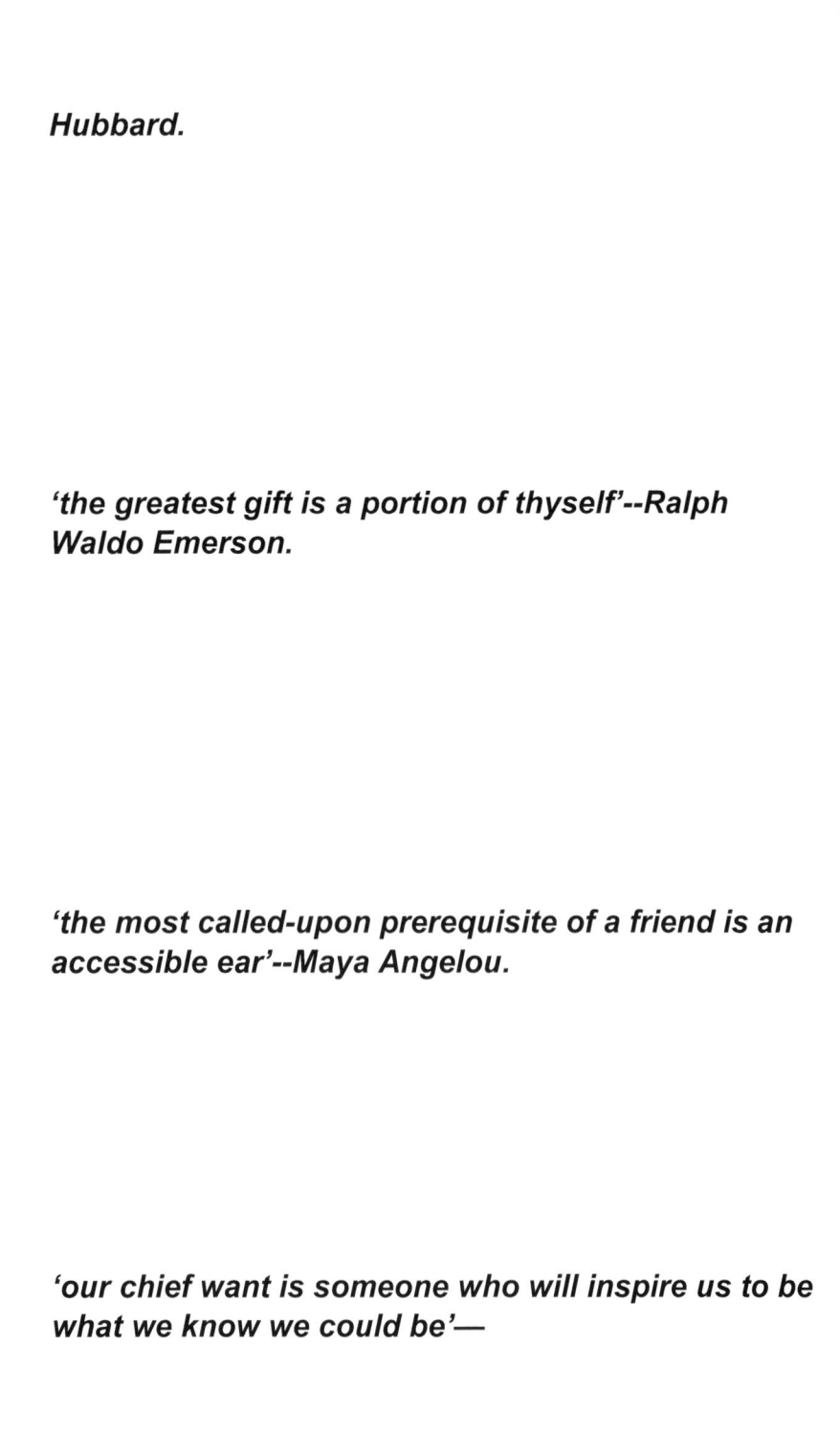

'the greatest gift is a portion of thyself'--Ralph Waldo Emerson.

'the most called-upon prerequisite of a friend is an accessible ear'--Maya Angelou.

'our chief want is someone who will inspire us to be what we know we could be'—

Ralph Waldo Emerson.

'be true to your work, your word, and your friend'--Henry David Thoreau.

'the best way to destroy an enemy is to make him a friend'--Abraham Lincoln.

'it takes a long time to grow an old friend'--John Leonard.

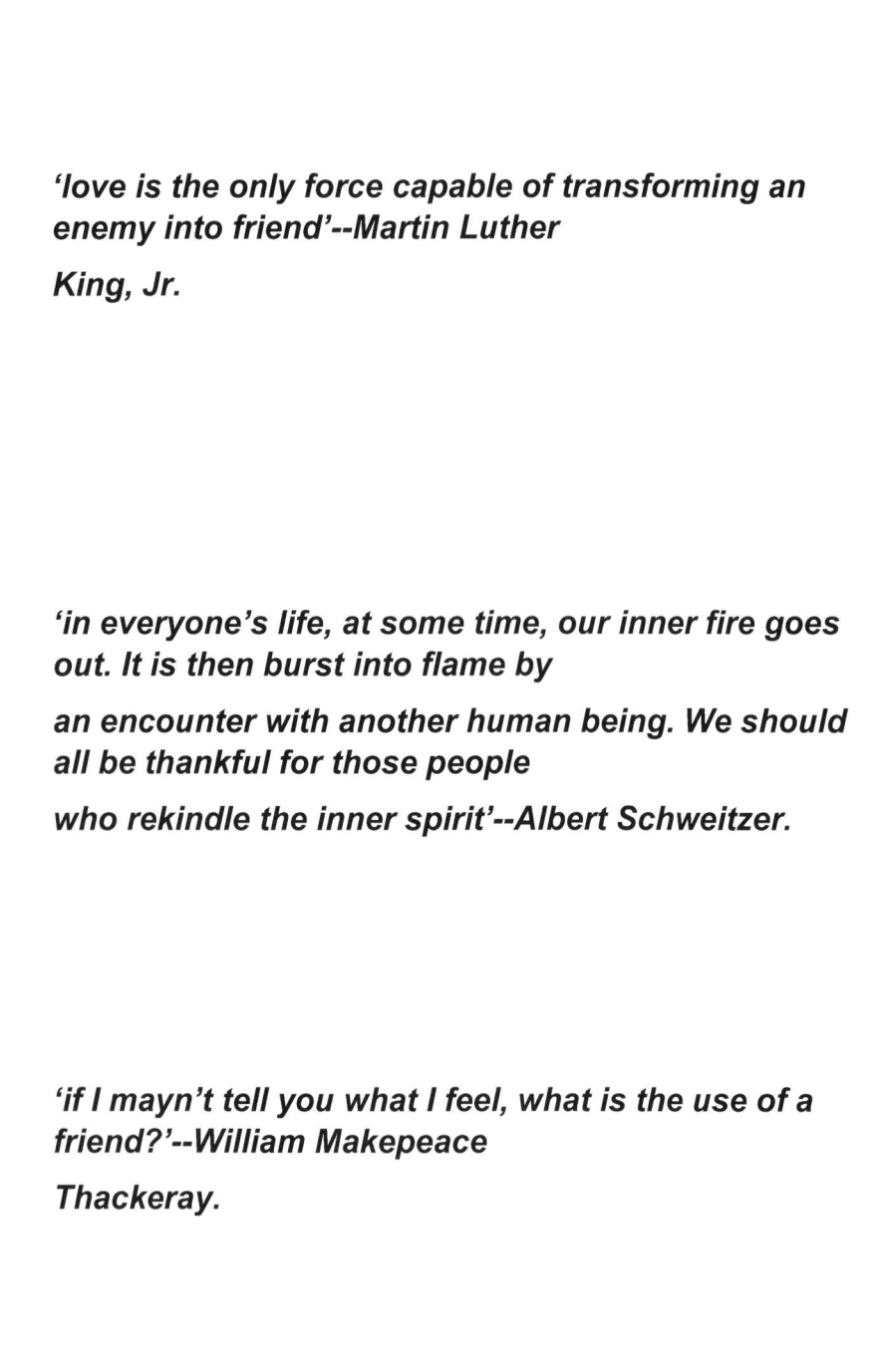

'love is the only force capable of transforming an enemy into friend'--Martin Luther King, Jr.

'in everyone's life, at some time, our inner fire goes out. It is then burst into flame by an encounter with another human being. We should all be thankful for those people who rekindle the inner spirit'--Albert Schweitzer.

'if I mayn't tell you what I feel, what is the use of a friend?'--William Makepeace Thackeray.

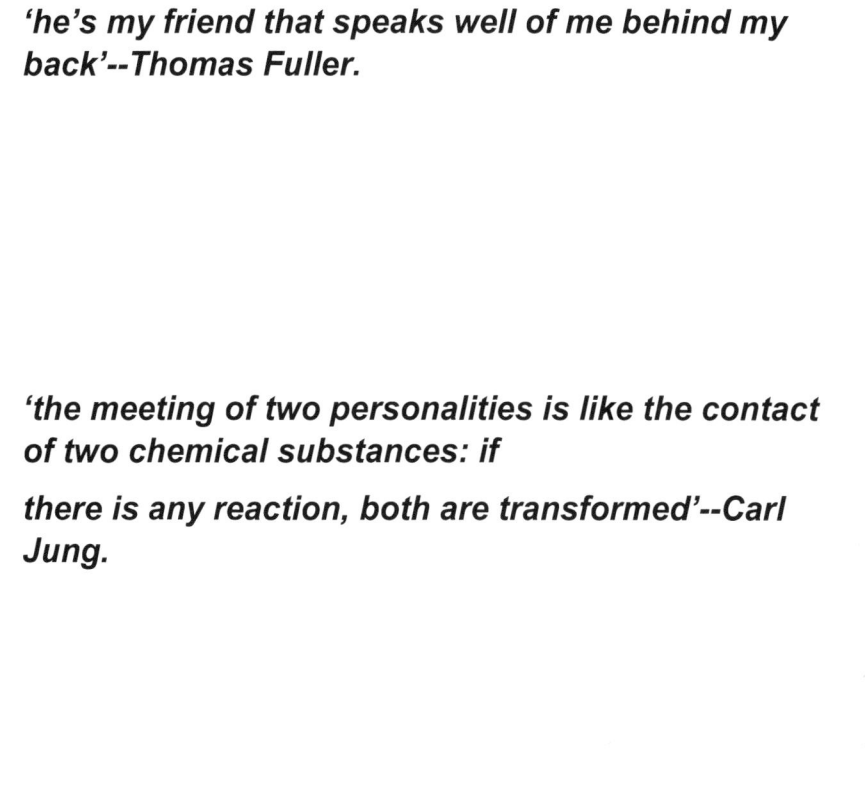

'he's my friend that speaks well of me behind my back'--Thomas Fuller.

'the meeting of two personalities is like the contact of two chemical substances: if

there is any reaction, both are transformed'--Carl Jung.

'We need to find god, and he cannot be found in noise and restlessness. God is the

friend of silence. See how nature- trees, flowers, grass, grows in silence; see the

stars, the moon and the sun, how they move in silence. We need silence to be able to

touch souls. --Mother Teresa.

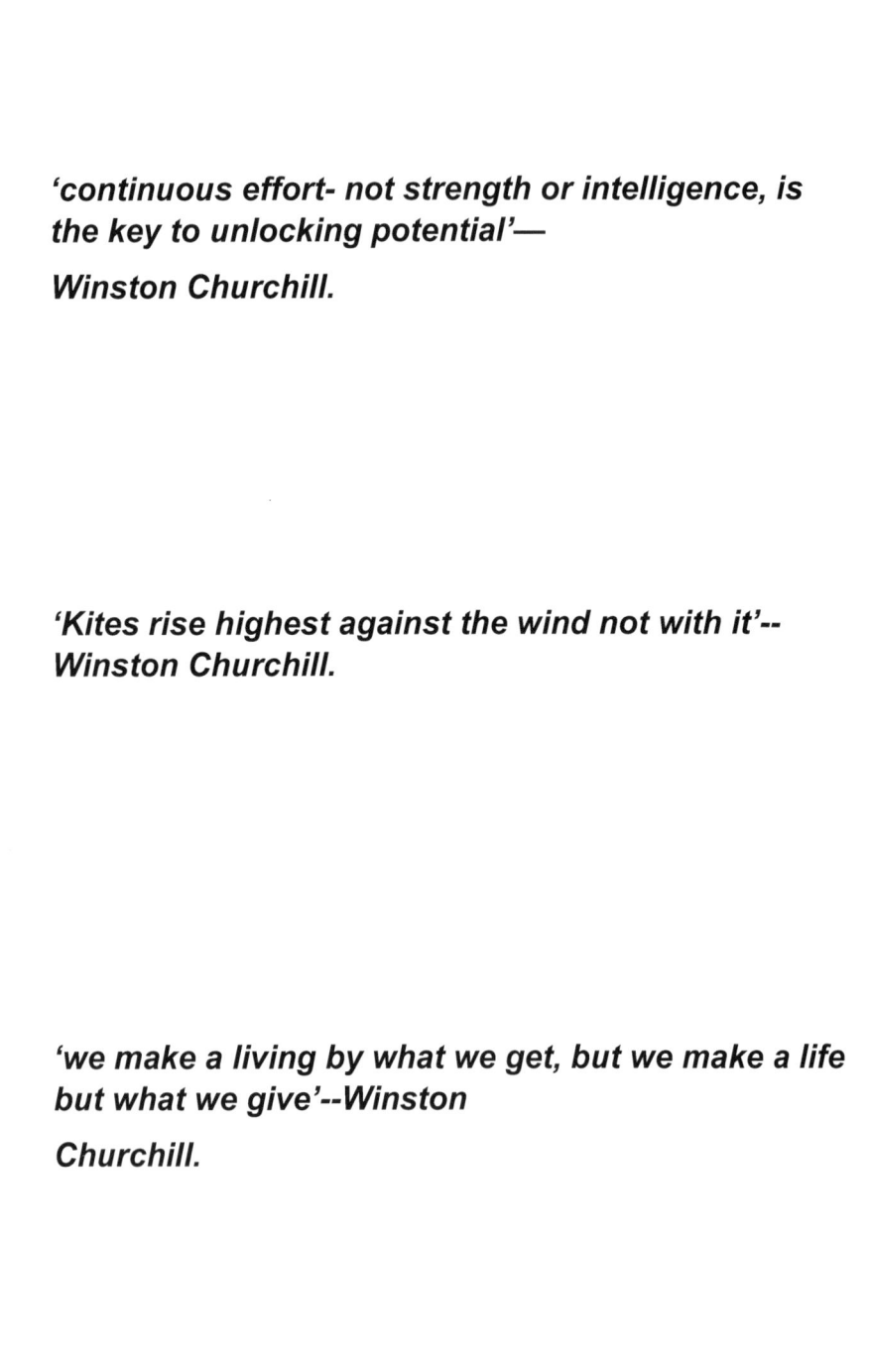

'continuous effort- not strength or intelligence, is the key to unlocking potential'—
Winston Churchill.

'Kites rise highest against the wind not with it'-- Winston Churchill.

'we make a living by what we get, but we make a life but what we give'--Winston
Churchill.

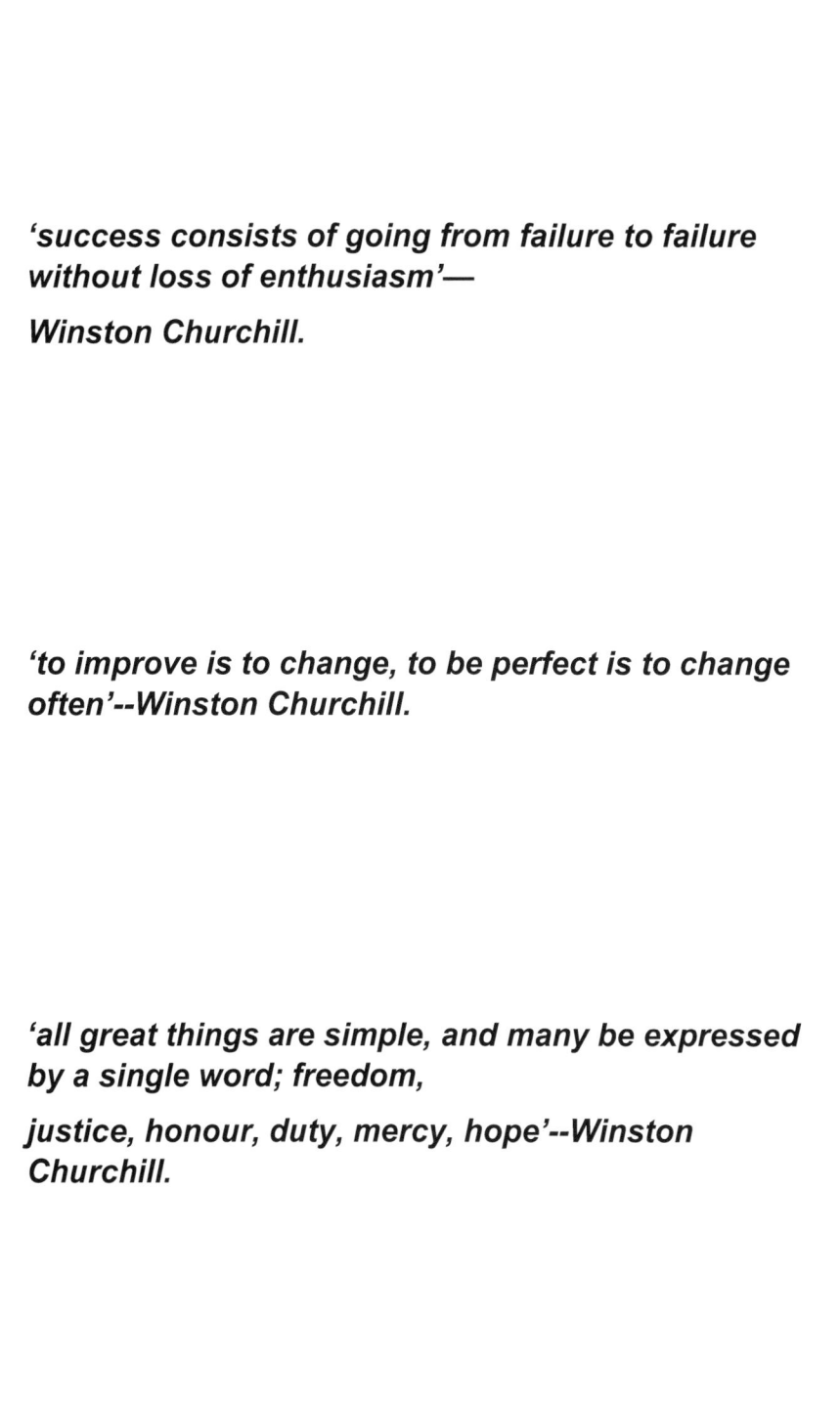

'success consists of going from failure to failure without loss of enthusiasm'—

Winston Churchill.

'to improve is to change, to be perfect is to change often'--Winston Churchill.

'all great things are simple, and many be expressed by a single word; freedom,

justice, honour, duty, mercy, hope'--Winston Churchill.

'for it is a fate of a woman, long to be patient and silent to wait like a ghost that is

speechless, till some questioning voice dissolves the spell of its distance'--Henry

Wadsworth Longfellow.

'the happiest moments my heart knows are these in which it is pouring forth its

affections to a few esteemed characters'--Thomas Jefferson.

'the most beautiful discovery true friends make is that they can grow separately without growing apart'--Elisabeth Foley.

'when you are alone you are not alone, you are simply lonely and there is a tremendous difference between loneliness and aloneness. When you are lonely you are thinking of the other, you are missing the other. Loneliness is a negative state. You are feeling that it would have been better if the other were there, your friend, your wife, your beloved, your husband. It would have been good if the other were there, but the other is not. Loneliness is absence of the other. Aloneness is the presence of oneself. Aloneness is very positive. It is presence, overflowing presence. You are so full of presence that you can fill the while universe with your presence and there is no need for anybody.--Osho.

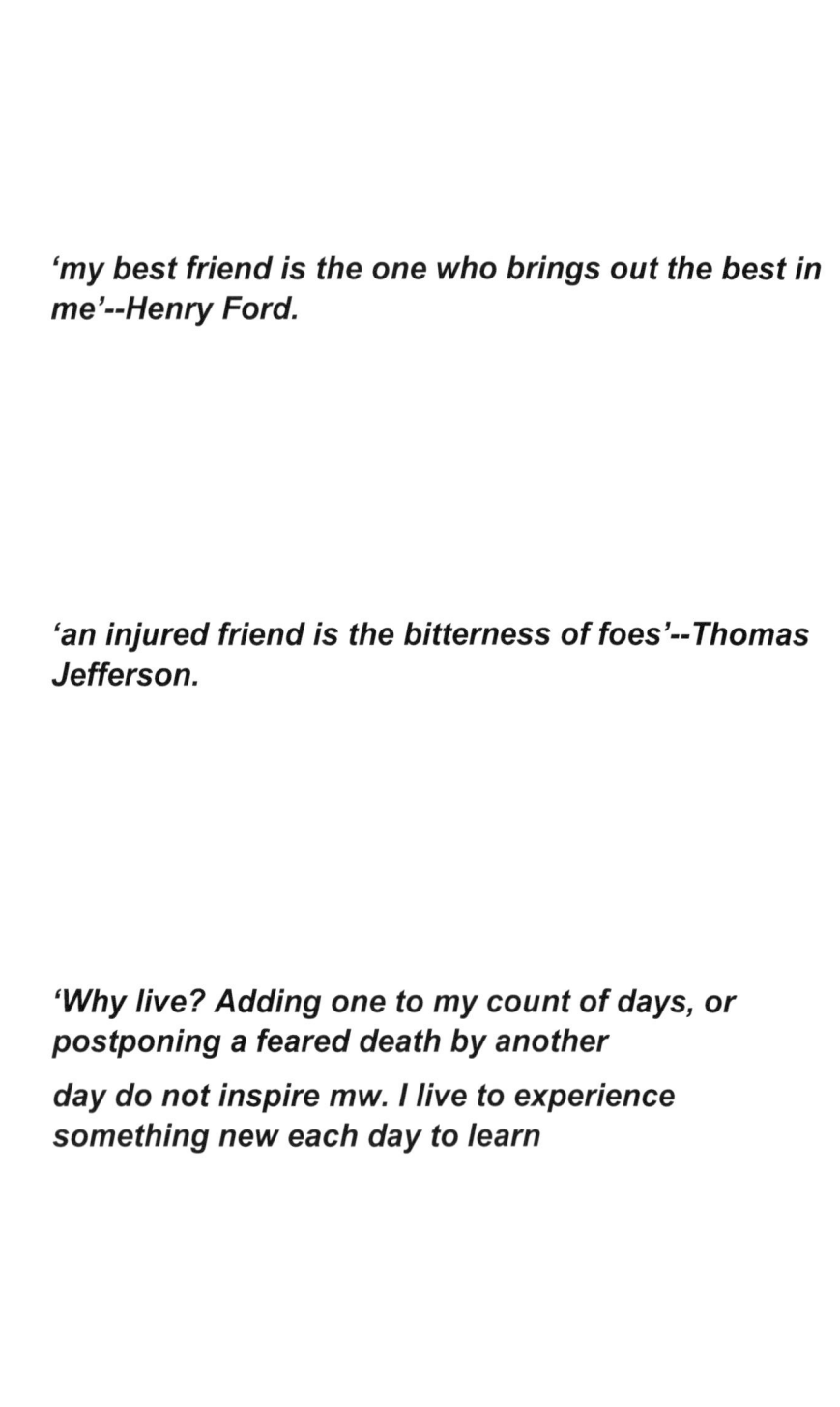

'my best friend is the one who brings out the best in me'--Henry Ford.

'an injured friend is the bitterness of foes'--Thomas Jefferson.

'Why live? Adding one to my count of days, or postponing a feared death by another

day do not inspire mw. I live to experience something new each day to learn *something new, meet a new friend, bring jot into someone's life, feel the wind newly*

on my skin, touch a new fear, a new anger, and with focused intent and good fortune,

find an ample measure of my own joy'--Jonathan Lockwood Huie.

'the only way to have a friend is to be one'--Ralph Waldo Emerson.

'the price of freedom for a nation is lives and money. Often, the price of freedom for

an individual is challenging the closed minds of family and friend'--Jonathan

Lockwood Huie.

'the walls we build around us to keep sadness out also keeps out the joy'--Jim Rohn.

'lord, grant comfort, joy and health to those I call friend, to those I call enemy, and to

those I have cursed by my indifference'--Jonathan Lockwood Huie.

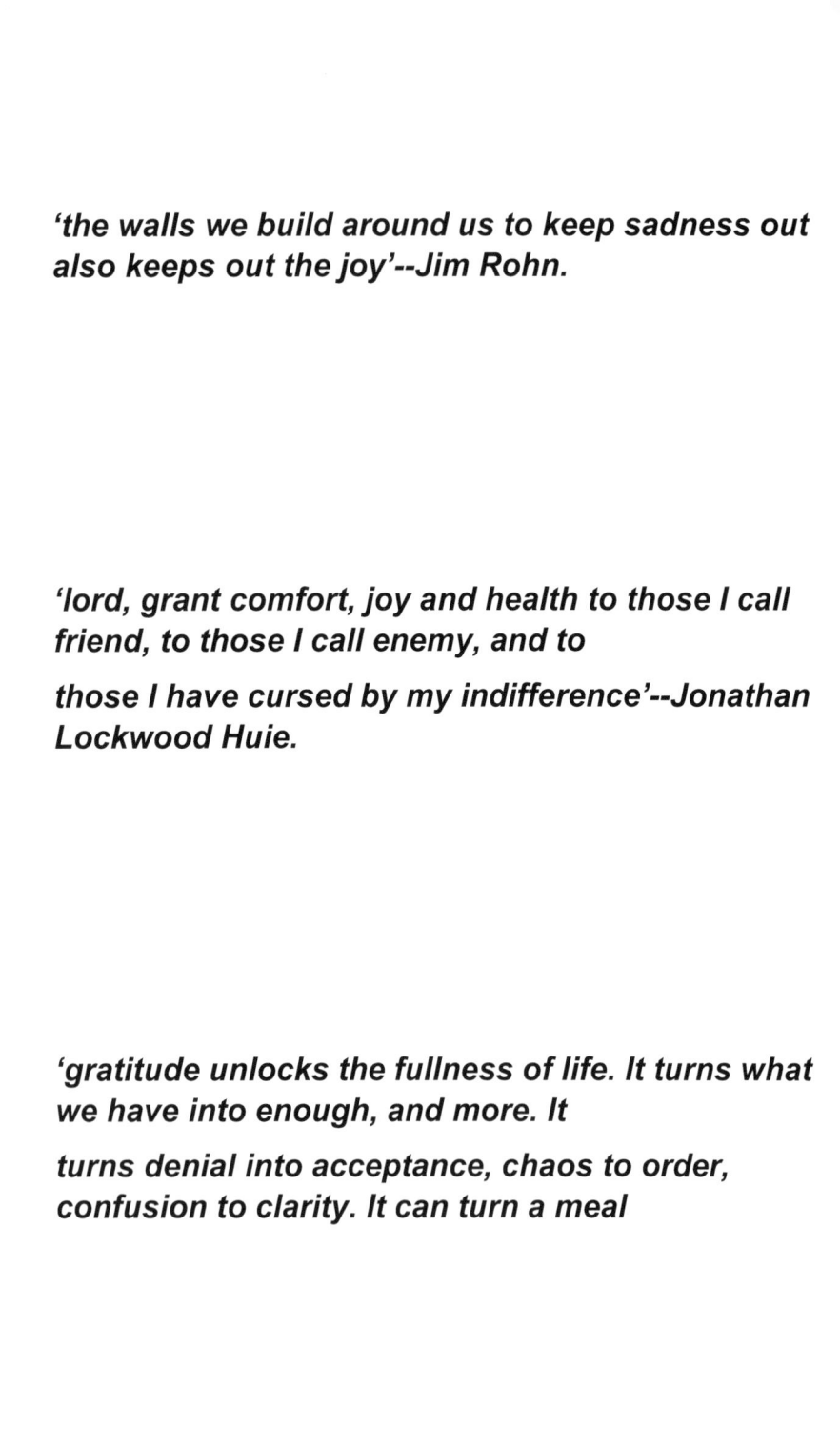

'gratitude unlocks the fullness of life. It turns what we have into enough, and more. It

turns denial into acceptance, chaos to order, confusion to clarity. It can turn a meal into a feast, a house into a home, a stranger into a friend. Gratitude makes sense of

our past, brings peace for today, and creates a vision for tomorrow'--Melody Beattie.

'I never found a companion that was so companionable as solitude'--Henry David

Thoreau.

'self-respect is often mistaken for arrogance when in reality it is the opposite. When

we can recognize all our good qualities as well as our faults with neutrality, we can

start to appreciate ourselves as we would a dear friend, and experience the

comfortable inner glow of respect. To embrace the journey towards our full potential we need to become our own loving teacher and coach. Spurring ourselves on to

become better human beings, we develop true regard for ourselves, and our life will

become sacred.--Osho.

'If you want to achieve greatness stop asking for permission'

'Things work out best for those who make the best of how things work out' --John Wooden

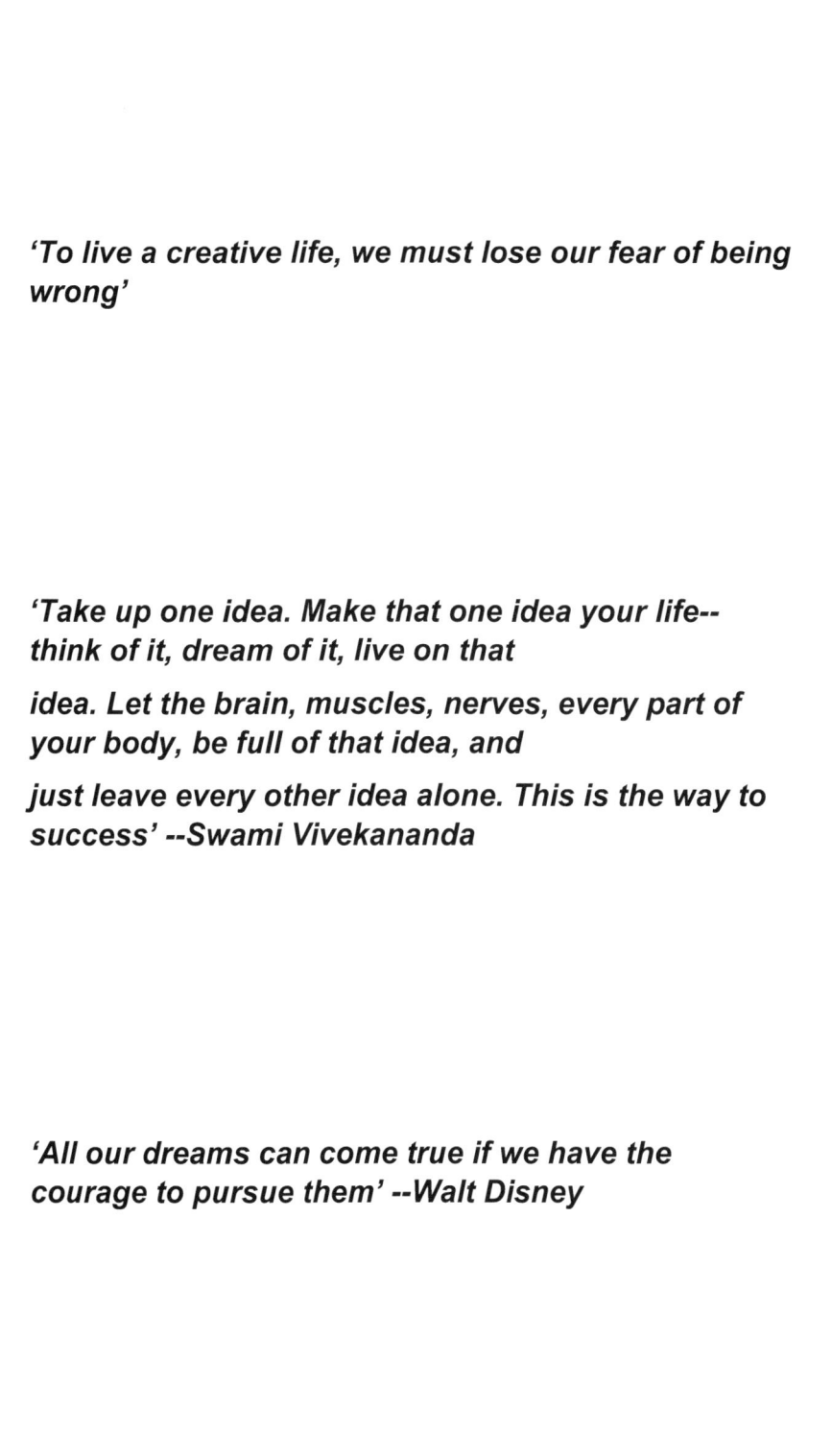

'To live a creative life, we must lose our fear of being wrong'

'Take up one idea. Make that one idea your life-- think of it, dream of it, live on that

idea. Let the brain, muscles, nerves, every part of your body, be full of that idea, and

just leave every other idea alone. This is the way to success' --Swami Vivekananda

'All our dreams can come true if we have the courage to pursue them' --Walt Disney

'If you do what you always did, you will get what you always got'

'Success is walking from failure to failure with no loss of enthusiasm'--Winston Churchill

'Just when the caterpillar thought the world was ending, he turned into a butterfly'

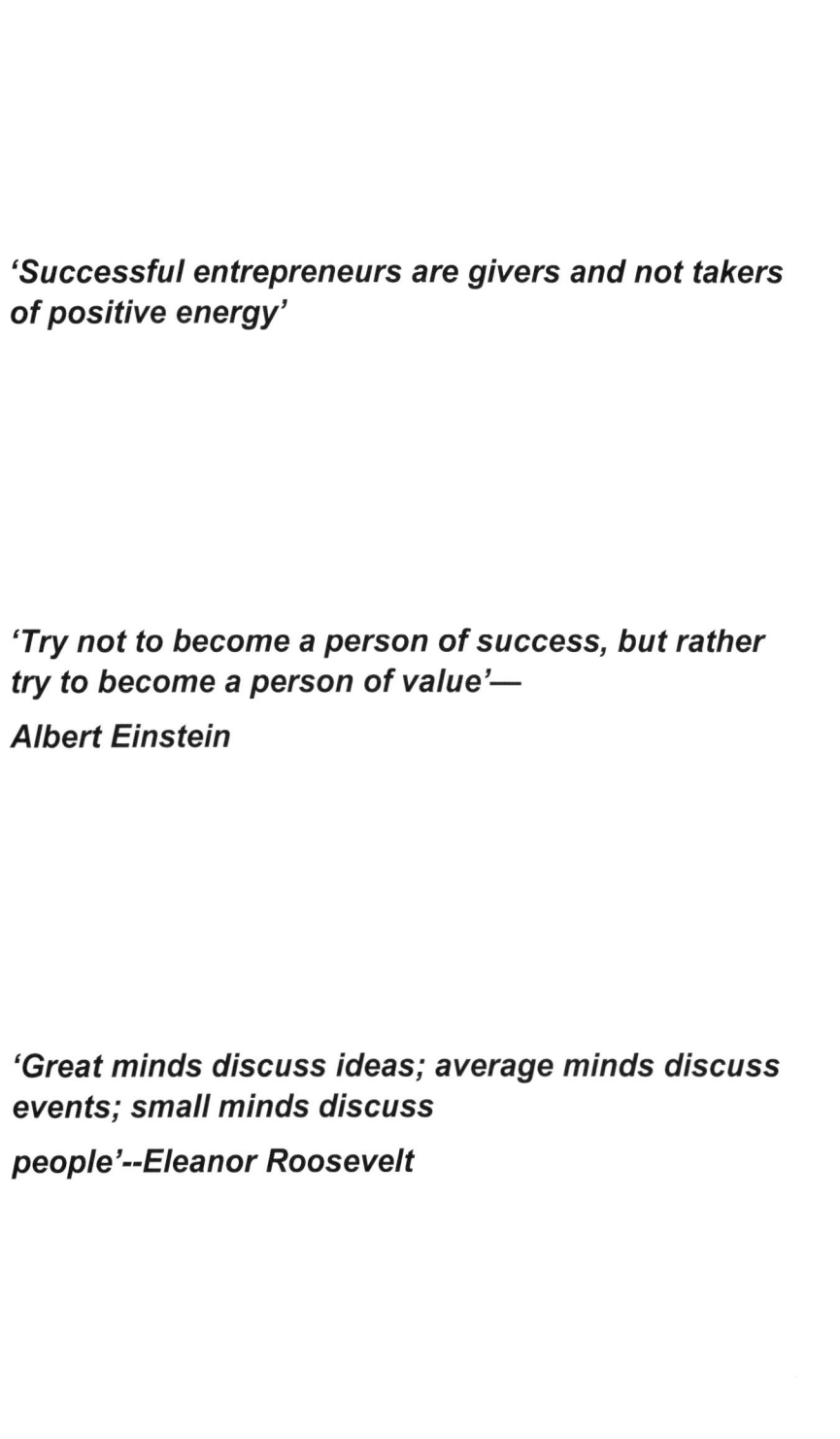

'Successful entrepreneurs are givers and not takers of positive energy'

'Try not to become a person of success, but rather try to become a person of value'—

Albert Einstein

'Great minds discuss ideas; average minds discuss events; small minds discuss

people'--Eleanor Roosevelt

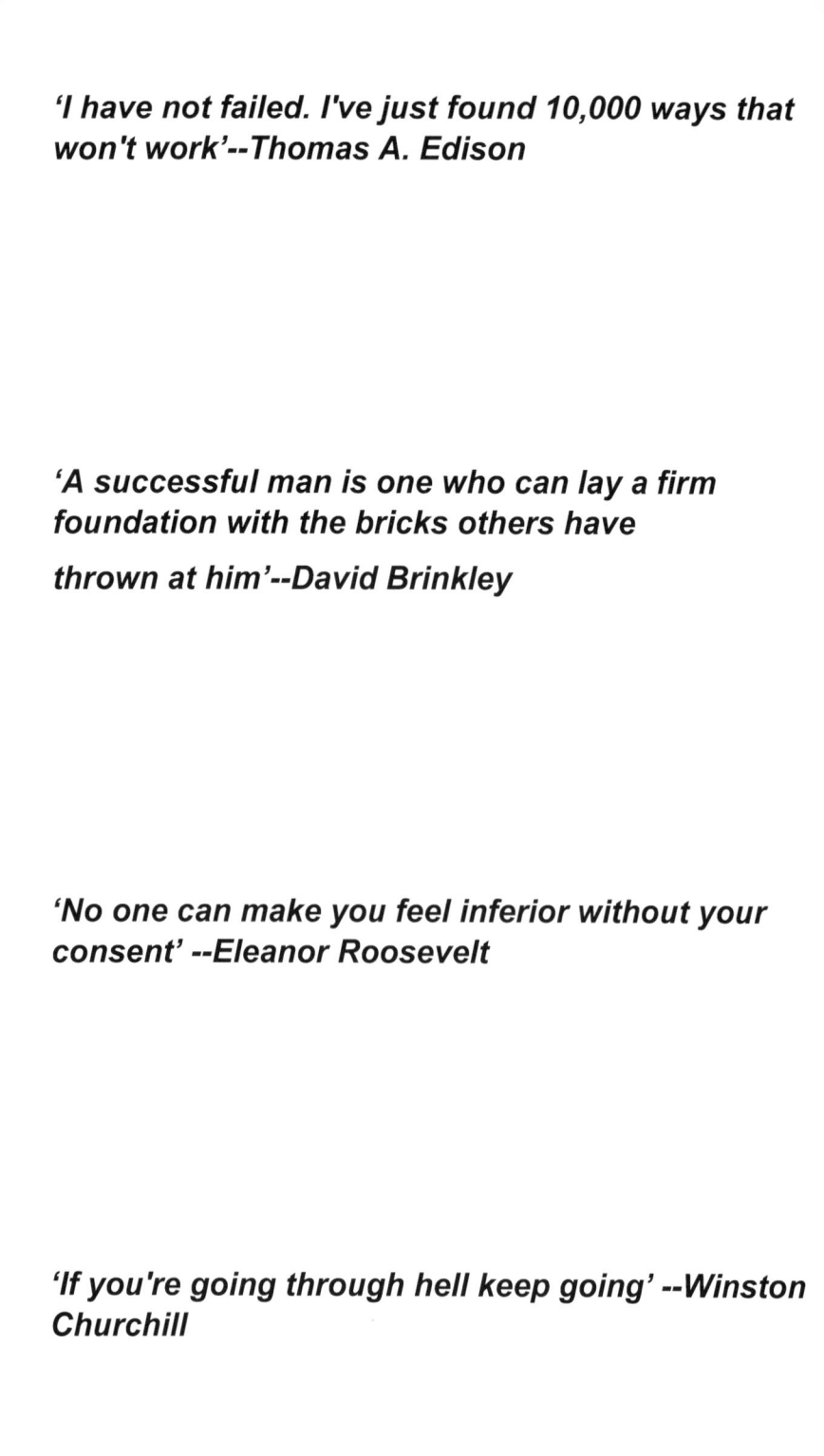

'I have not failed. I've just found 10,000 ways that won't work'--Thomas A. Edison

'A successful man is one who can lay a firm foundation with the bricks others have thrown at him'--David Brinkley

'No one can make you feel inferior without your consent' --Eleanor Roosevelt

'If you're going through hell keep going' --Winston Churchill

'The ones who are crazy enough to think they can change the world, are the ones who do'

"What seems to us as bitter trials are often blessings in disguise." --Oscar Wilde

The meaning of life is to find your gift. The purpose of life is to give it away."

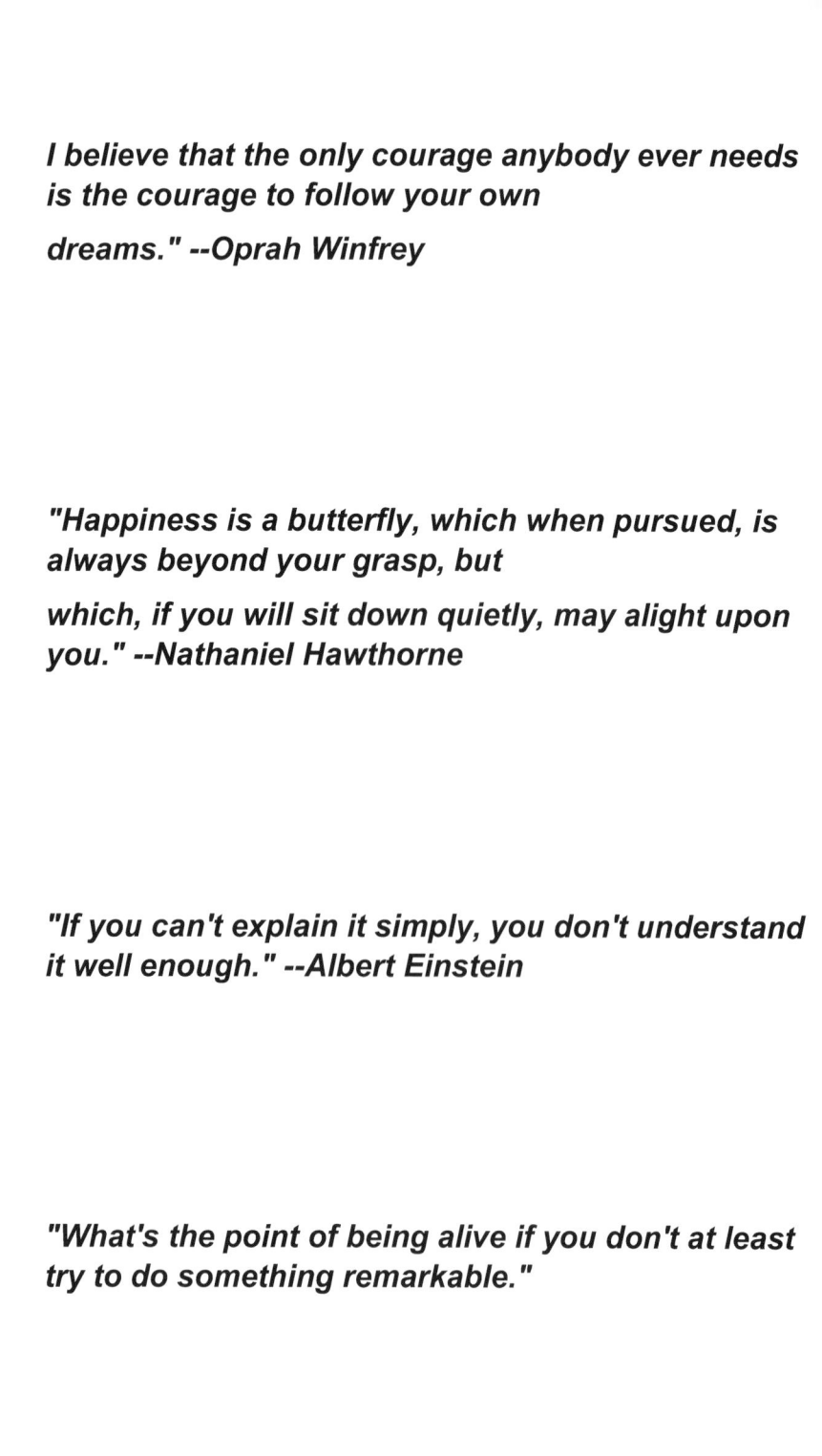

I believe that the only courage anybody ever needs is the courage to follow your own dreams." --Oprah Winfrey

"Happiness is a butterfly, which when pursued, is always beyond your grasp, but

which, if you will sit down quietly, may alight upon you." --Nathaniel Hawthorne

"If you can't explain it simply, you don't understand it well enough." --Albert Einstein

"What's the point of being alive if you don't at least try to do something remarkable."

"Life is not about finding yourself. Life is about creating yourself." --Lolly Daskal

"There are two types of people who will tell you that you cannot make a difference in

this world: those who are afraid to try and those who are afraid you will succeed." –

Ray Goforth

"I find that the harder I work; the more luck I seem to have." --Thomas Jefferson

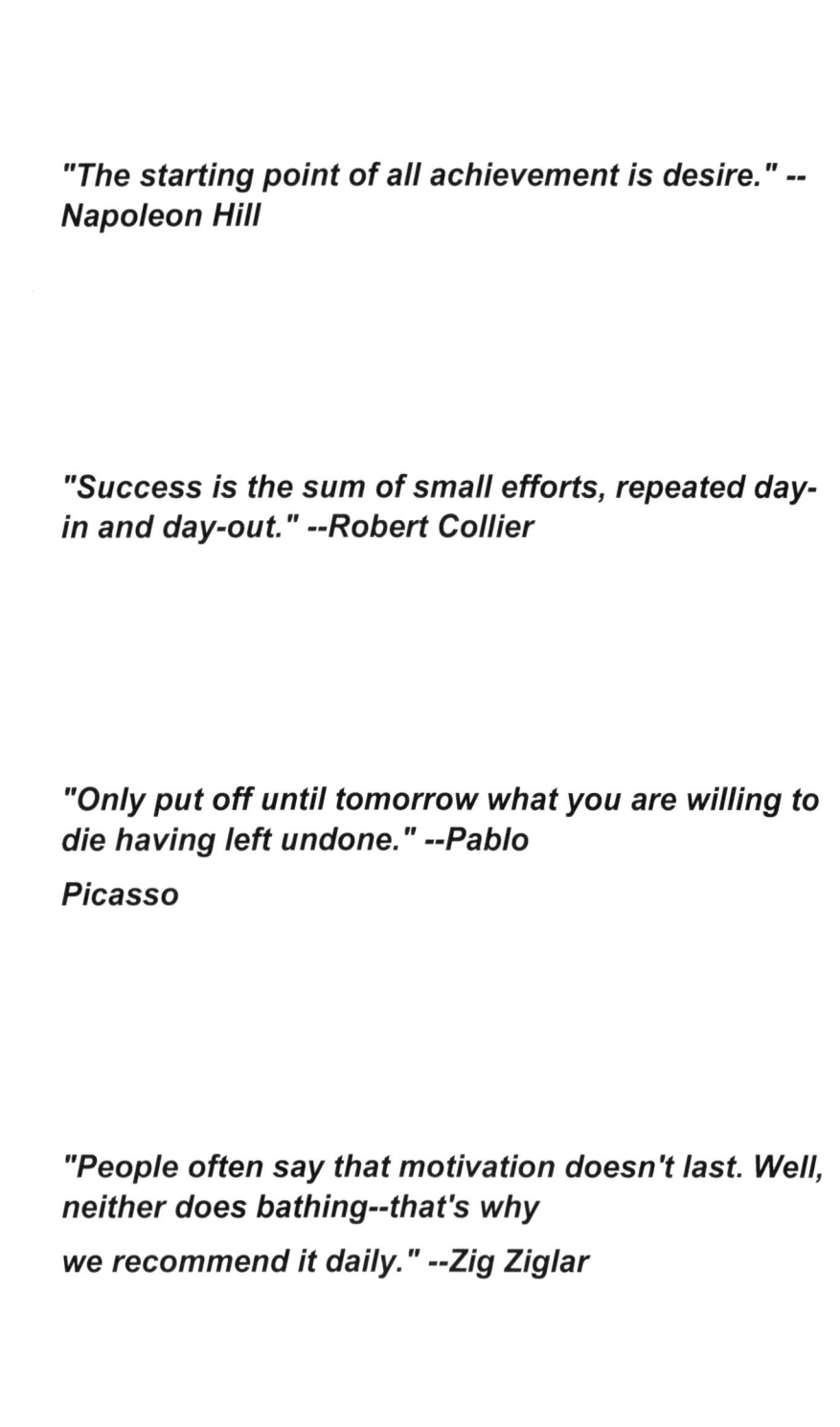

"The starting point of all achievement is desire." --Napoleon Hill

"Success is the sum of small efforts, repeated day-in and day-out." --Robert Collier

"Only put off until tomorrow what you are willing to die having left undone." --Pablo Picasso

"People often say that motivation doesn't last. Well, neither does bathing--that's why we recommend it daily." --Zig Ziglar

"We become what we think about most of the time, and that's the strangest secret." – Earl Nightingale

"The only place where success comes before work is in the dictionary." --Vidal Sassoon

"Too many of us are not living our dreams because we are living our fears. " --Les Brown

"I find that when you have a real interest in life and a curious life, that sleep is not the most important thing." --Martha Stewart

"The function of leadership is to produce more leaders, not more followers." --Ralph Nader

"As we look ahead into the next century, leaders will be those who empower others." –
-Bill Gates

"The first step toward success is taken when you refuse to be a captive of the

environment in which you first find yourself." --Mark Caine

"People who succeed have momentum. The more they succeed, the more they want

to succeed, and the more they find a way to succeed. Similarly, when someone is

failing, the tendency is to get on a downward spiral that can even become a self-

fulfilling prophecy." --Tony Robbins

"When I dare to be powerful, to use my strength in the service of my vision, then it

becomes less and less important whether I am afraid." --Audre Lorde

"The successful warrior is the average man, with laser-like focus." --Bruce Lee

"Develop success from failures. Discouragement and failure are two of the surest

stepping stones to success." --Dale Carnegie

"Don't let the fear of losing be greater than the excitement of winning." --Robert

Kiyosaki

"The number one reason people fail in life is because they listen to their friends,

family, and neighbours." --Napoleon Hill

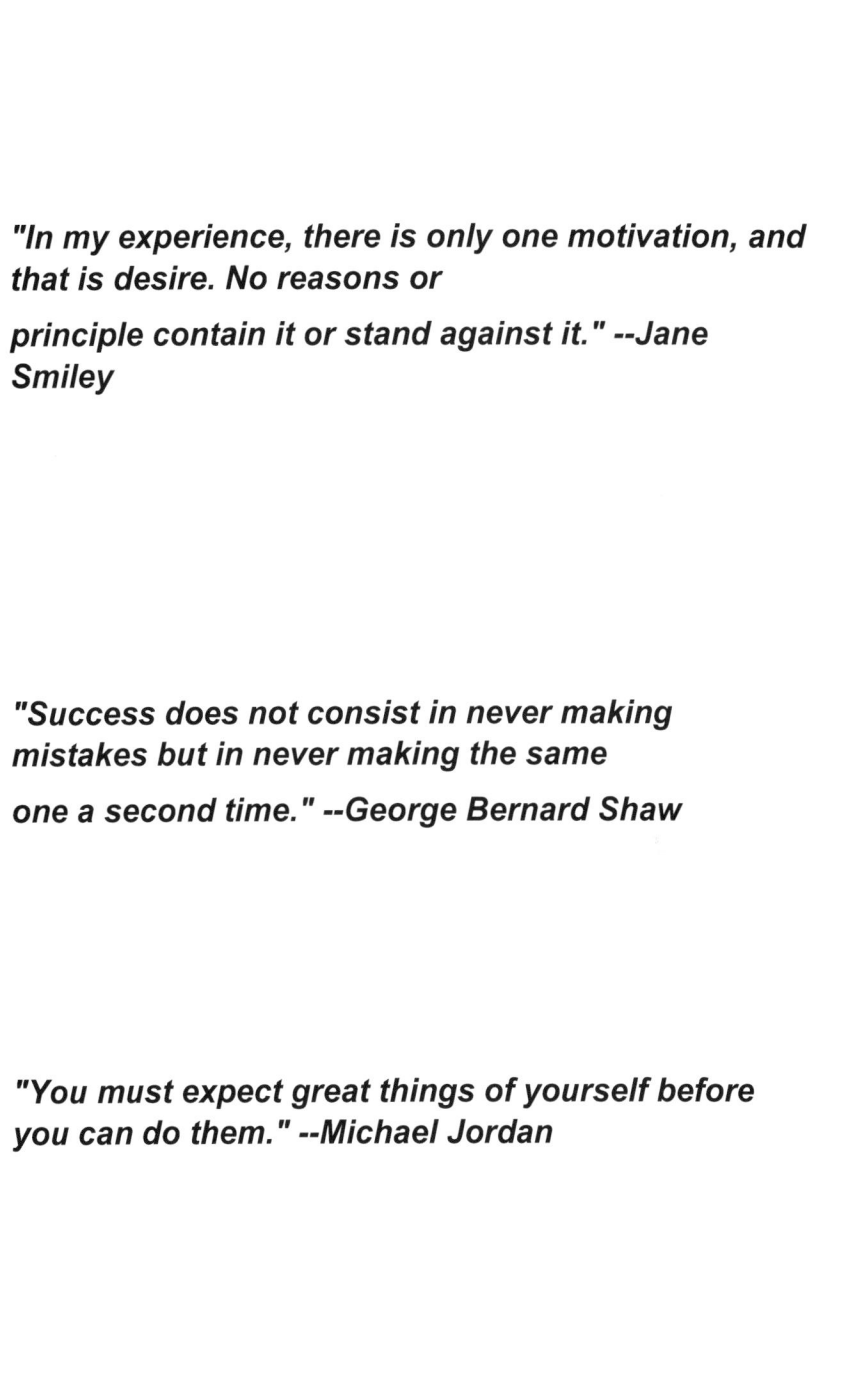

"In my experience, there is only one motivation, and that is desire. No reasons or principle contain it or stand against it." --Jane Smiley

"Success does not consist in never making mistakes but in never making the same one a second time." --George Bernard Shaw

"You must expect great things of yourself before you can do them." --Michael Jordan

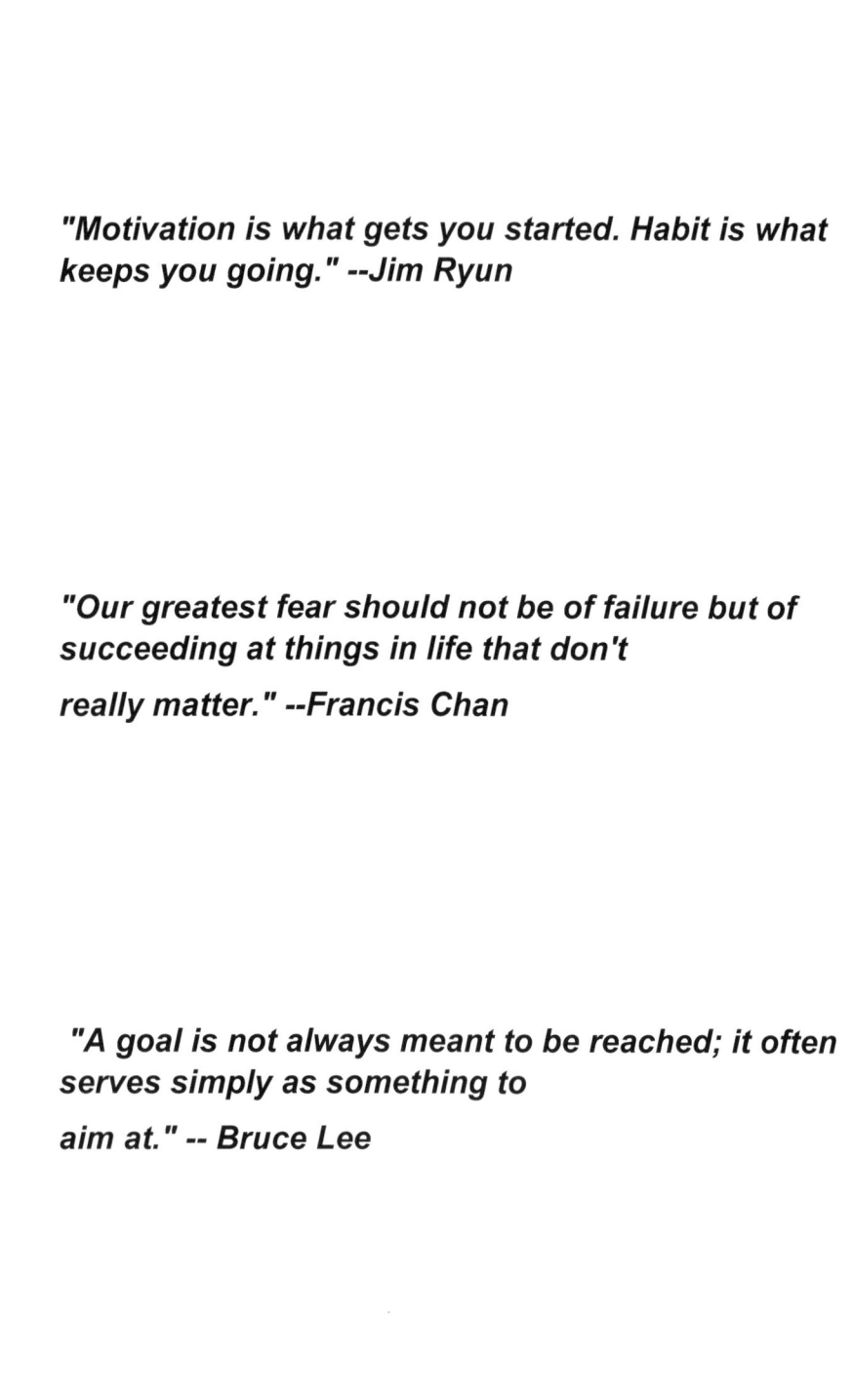

"Motivation is what gets you started. Habit is what keeps you going." --Jim Ryun

"Our greatest fear should not be of failure but of succeeding at things in life that don't really matter." --Francis Chan

"A goal is not always meant to be reached; it often serves simply as something to aim at." -- Bruce Lee

"To accomplish great things, we must not only act, but also dream, not only plan, but also believe." --Anatole France

"Most of the important things in the world have been accomplished by people who have kept on trying when there seemed to be no help at all." --Dale Carnegie

"Real difficulties can be overcome; it is only the imaginary ones that are unconquerable." --Theodore N. Vail

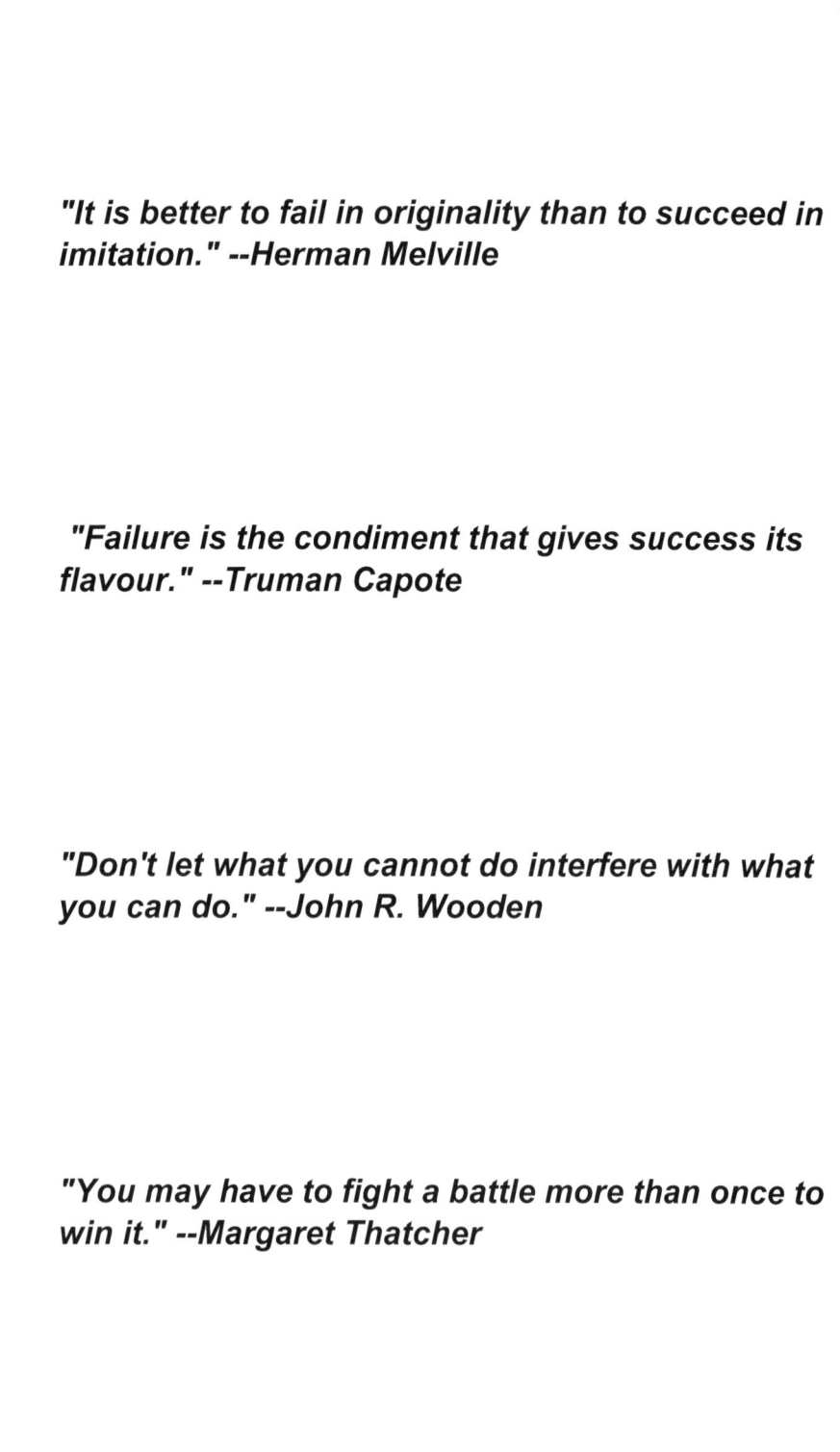

"It is better to fail in originality than to succeed in imitation." --Herman Melville

"Failure is the condiment that gives success its flavour." --Truman Capote

"Don't let what you cannot do interfere with what you can do." --John R. Wooden

"You may have to fight a battle more than once to win it." --Margaret Thatcher

"A man can be as great as he wants to be. If you believe in yourself and have the courage, the determination, the dedication, the competitive drive and if you are willing to sacrifice the little things in life and pay the price for the things that are worthwhile, it can be done." --Vince Lombardi

'The Journey of a thousand miles, begins with just one step'--Lao Tzo

'change your thoughts and you change your world'

'no act of kindness, however small is ever wasted'

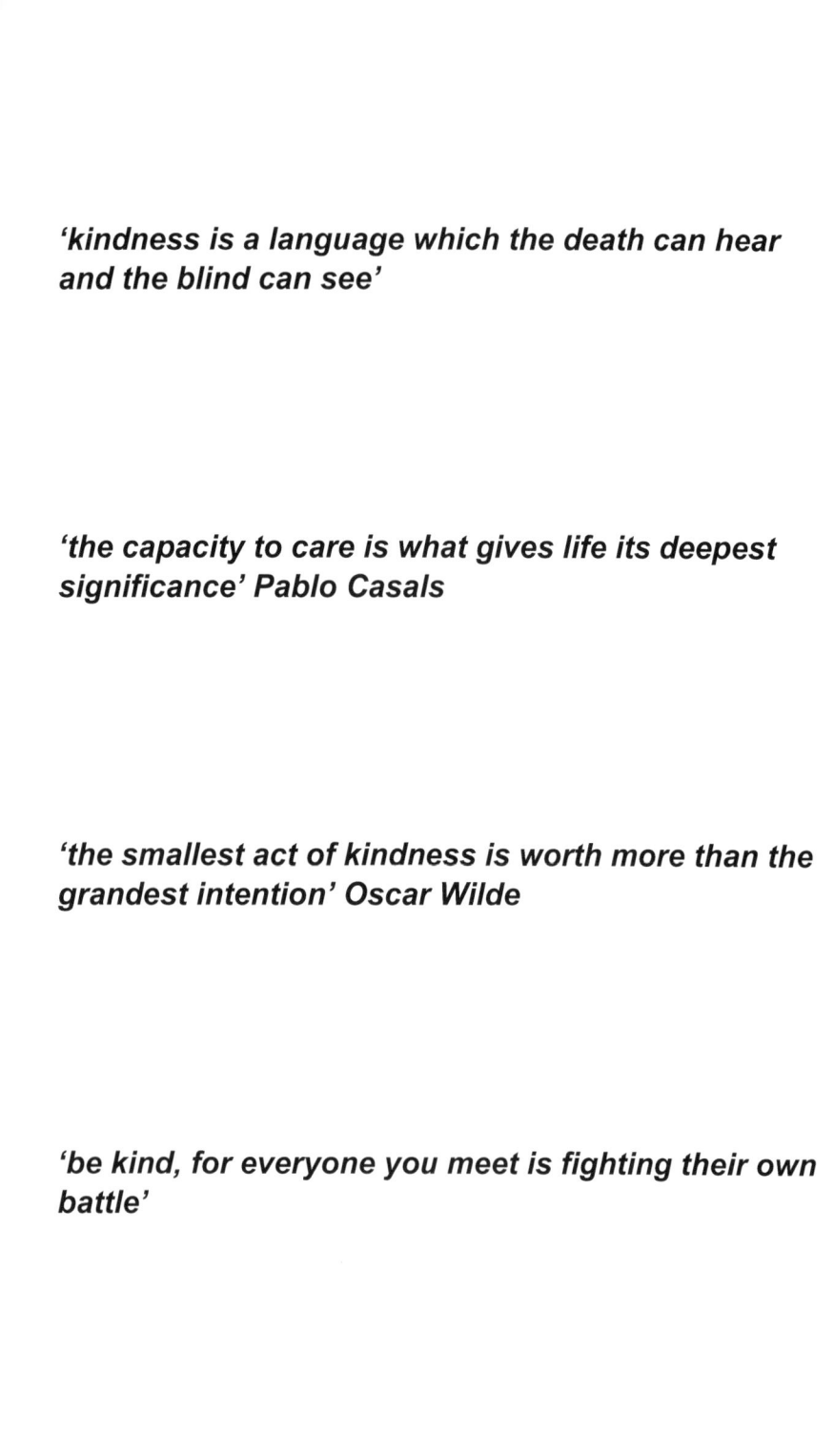

'kindness is a language which the death can hear and the blind can see'

'the capacity to care is what gives life its deepest significance' Pablo Casals

'the smallest act of kindness is worth more than the grandest intention' Oscar Wilde

'be kind, for everyone you meet is fighting their own battle' *'the best portion of a good man's life; his little, nameless unremembered acts of*

kindness and love' William Wordsworth.

'kindness is more important than wisdom, and the recognition of this is the beginning

of wisdom' Theodore Rubin.

'kind words can be short and easy to speak, but their echoes are truly endless'

Mother Teresa.

'kindness is not weakness; it truly is strength'

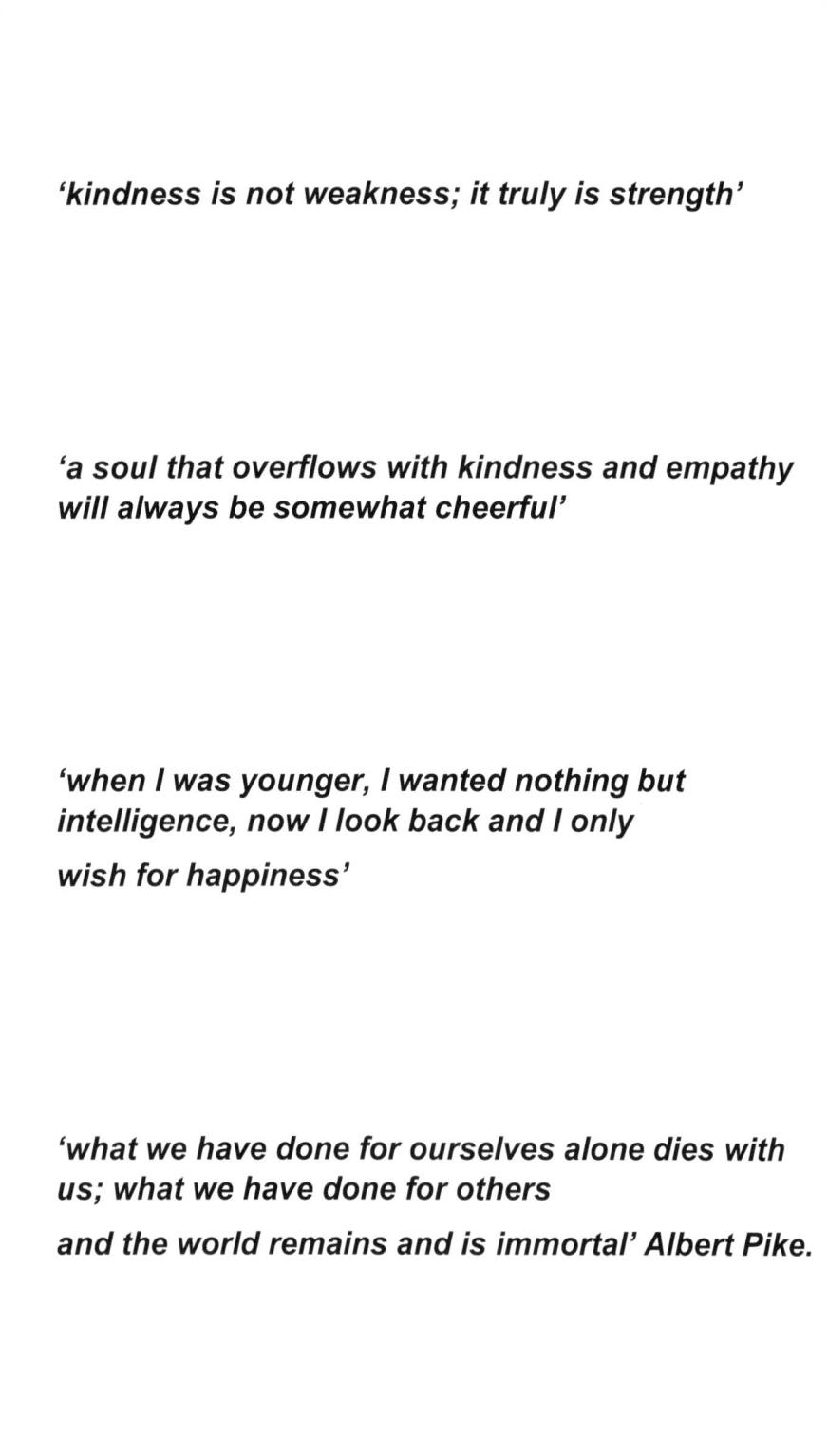

'a soul that overflows with kindness and empathy will always be somewhat cheerful'

'when I was younger, I wanted nothing but intelligence, now I look back and I only wish for happiness'

'what we have done for ourselves alone dies with us; what we have done for others and the world remains and is immortal' **Albert Pike.**

'do not wait to be kind, because if you wait you may miss your chance'

'for beautiful eyes, look for the good in others; for beautiful lips, speak only words of

kindness; and for poise, walk with knowledge that you are never alone' Audrey

Hepburn.

'we think too much and feel too little. More than machinery, we need humanity. More

than cleverness, we need kindness and gentleness' Charlie Chaplin.

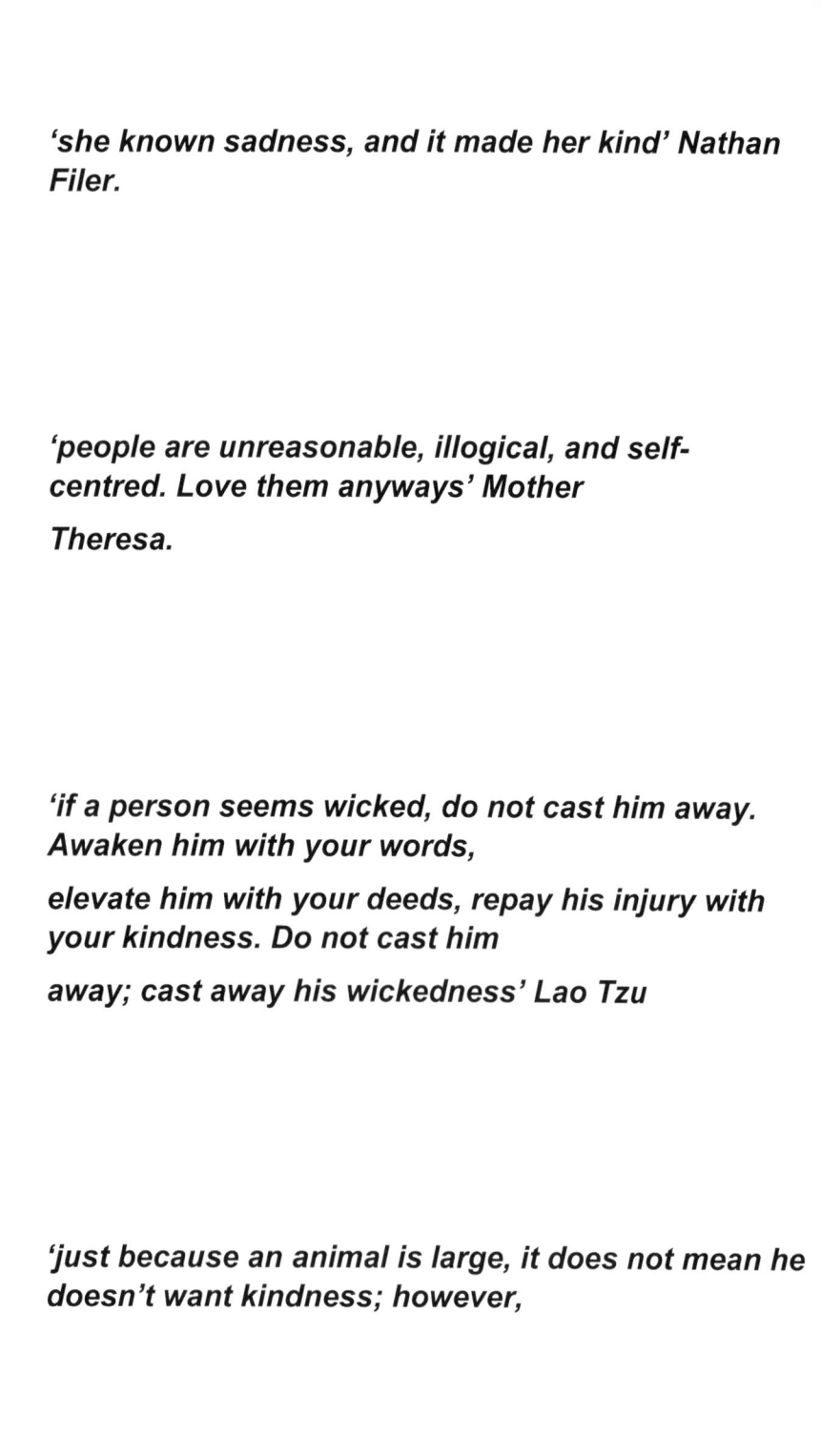

'she known sadness, and it made her kind' Nathan Filer.

'people are unreasonable, illogical, and self-centred. Love them anyways' Mother Theresa.

'if a person seems wicked, do not cast him away. Awaken him with your words,

elevate him with your deeds, repay his injury with your kindness. Do not cast him

away; cast away his wickedness' Lao Tzu

'just because an animal is large, it does not mean he doesn't want kindness; however,

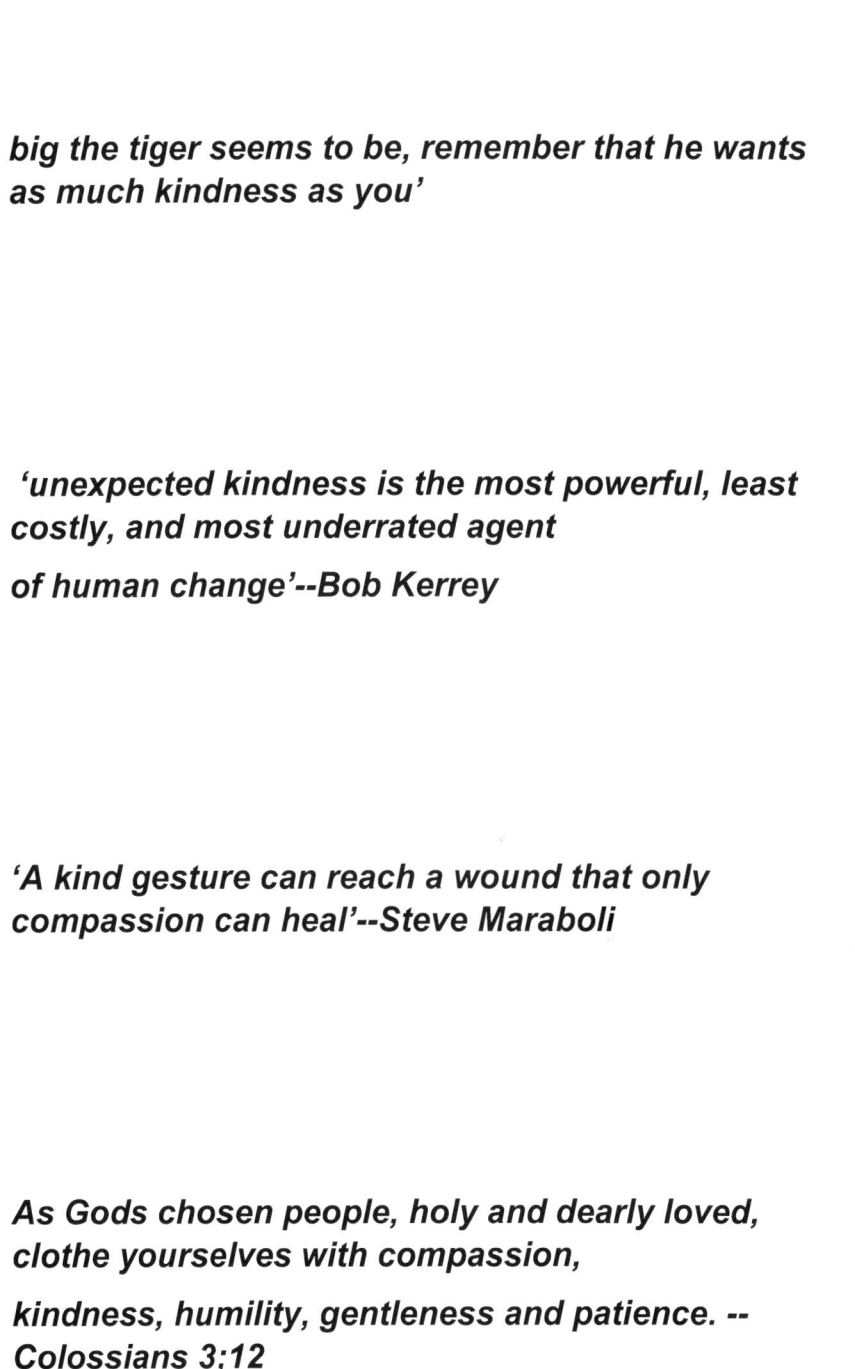

big the tiger seems to be, remember that he wants as much kindness as you'

'unexpected kindness is the most powerful, least costly, and most underrated agent

of human change'--Bob Kerrey

'A kind gesture can reach a wound that only compassion can heal'--Steve Maraboli

As Gods chosen people, holy and dearly loved, clothe yourselves with compassion,

kindness, humility, gentleness and patience. -- Colossians 3;12

'never lose a chance of saying a kind word'--William Makepeace Thackeray.

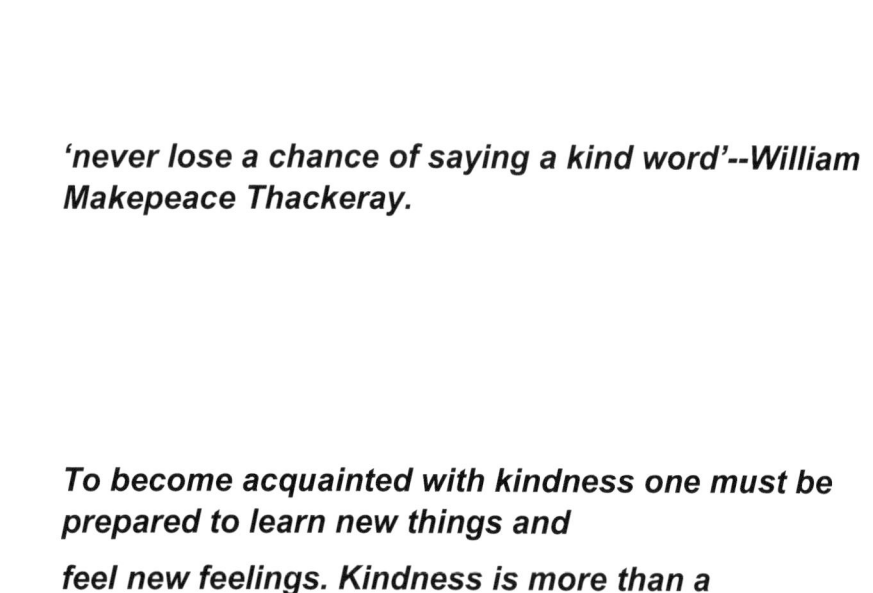

To become acquainted with kindness one must be prepared to learn new things and

feel new feelings. Kindness is more than a philosophy of the mins. It is a philosophy

of the spirit'--Robert J. Furel

Summaries

Thoughts are the hardest thing to take control over. Thoughts are a built habit over the years, thoughts are the words that have been spoken to you, for all those years. Without thinking, we think the same thoughts over and over. We need to try and change each thought, although tough it can be done. We need to be kind and say kind words to each other. We need to be positive not just for ourselves for others. The more positive a life becomes the happier each individual is around this life. Say only kind words to each other, if you have nothing nice to say, then it is best not to say it at all.

The best way to predict our future is to invent it, yes our future does not yet exist, so it is possible to invent our new future ourselves. We have all the control if we really want it. What sort of future would you like to see, because I personally would love to see a peaceful and kind world? We all want a future we are happy with. Let's work together as a world to enable a better future for mankind.

The price of your time with another human being, should not be taken for granted. Time is all we have left in this world after kindness. Why make your time slow and hard when you can make it satisfying, kind, loving and peaceful?

Everything we as human beings own materially, has been accomplished by mankind. It was a dream for someone, who made it real. The real survivors in our world are those whom follow their dreams with actions. My dream cannot be made; my dream cannot only be learned. My dream is to motivate, encourage and spread kindness. If you are unsure of your purpose in this world, just ensure you remain kind and level headed, and when you find solitude and peace inside, then will you find your true dreams and aspirations.

Many are afraid to leave their comfort zone, due to the unknown being scary. It is best sometimes to leave your comfort zone as the unknown is where life is created, and can be fun. It is fine to stumble along whilst you venture forth and leaving the familiar behind you. Do not remain still no matter the trouble ahead for sure, soon you will find the unknown a comfort and the more successful you shall become.

Not all success has become from luck, those who seem lucky may have just left their comfort zone and worked hard. Luck has been described as the moment when preparation meets opportunity, with that being said, you have to put in the work to get prepared for once opportunity presents its self and be prepared to grasp those opportunities'. Therefore, we cannot take advantage of luck at any moment. Be prepared to put in the work and the opportunity's will arise.

A dream inhales small goals, although a goal may not seem like much, your overall dream will be. A goal may seem as though you are doing nothing, this may lay especially true of any outsider's view. This is where you need to have the confidence in the direction you are going. You need to have a clear dream to have conviction that the small steps you take, will eventually get you to where you want to end up.

Whenever we have a dream, our thoughts take over our minds, we feel afraid of failure and we keep our dreams on a leash. However, to overcome that fear and keep heading towards your dream, without standing still, your mind will remain to inhabit new goals along your journey to success. You may fail with particular routes you have taking towards your goal, but if you remain to move forward you will eventually find the correct route towards your dream. Failure comes with trying, and a life of not trying at all, will not leave you satisfied.

It is true that words we use can more than often be a contradiction of the actions we take. Words are far too easily thrown around and actions are more of a mundane task. Actions entail more thought and a more accurate measure of what is truly your intention, actions should be chosen wisely as humans now take actions as clarity more than a mere word. What we do matters more than what we say, but still remain with words of kindness and empathy.

It's easy to get frustrated by all the violence and pain being experienced around the world, and even easier to feel helpless about it. But rather than sitting around waiting for the world to change, it's better to start making changes within your own sphere of influence. The theory behind this quote is that if everyone tended to their own selves the world would be the way we all want it to be. What can you do today that would help make the world around you a better place? By making the changes you wish the world would make you instantly and automatically make the world better.

It's true that even the toughest of times don't last forever, and as long as you remain strong you'll make it through and be able to weather whatever storms come your way. The human spirit has shown that it's capable of making it through tough times, and getting to the end of the tunnel. The best part of dealing with adversity is that it toughens you up for the next trial in your life. Knowing that you're only getting better with each new struggle can be an inspiration during those times when you feel like giving up. Being a tough person doesn't mean you have to be callous, it just means you have an inner strength that's battle-tested.

As long as you're looking on the bright side of things you'll be ignoring the not-so-good things in your life. What you give attention to grows, so if you're focusing on what's wrong in your life you'll just get more of it to focus on. But if you focus on what's right in your life, what makes you happy, what you're grateful for, and why things are so fantastic for you, you'll only get more of the same to be happy and grateful for. Some days are easier to face towards the sunshine than others, but it's always there, you just have to try harder during hard times.

It's your life, your one and only life, and it would be a shame to spend it in a way that doesn't suit you. But many of us wish that things were different. Either we're unsatisfied with our jobs, or our relationships, or just the way things are going. It's vital to your overall success to make changes as you see fit so that you can have your life be the way you really want it to be. It's the foundation to all other success, and you can't really have a different success without first tending to this matter.

If you're in a tough spot it's tempting to think of a clever way around it, but this serves as a reminder to just take the most direct route: through. You'll find that a funny thing happens when you make up your mind to barrel through whatever dilemma you're facing. Everything starts shifting when you stop hemming and hawing and finally decide to take actions to make your way through. It's a way to get yourself on board with the idea of sticking it out and making it through, and when you stop the internal bickering you start to use your full potential to solve the problem at hand.

You use your imagination each day, even if you think you don't. No matter how big or small your accomplishments today, it all began in your imagination. You can use it as much or as little as you want, but it's the starting point for everything that happens in your life, from what you eat, to what you wear, to what you do. It all begins as pictures in your mind. Be sure to harness the full power of your imagination to dream up bigger and better things for yourself. It's the part of you that taps into the infiniteness of the universe, so don't neglect it.

It's easy to lose sight of the importance of each day, because we seem to have so many of them. But it's been said that a single day serves as a microcosm of your life, so be sure to spend your days in a way that embodies the way you want to live your life. At the end of it all your life will boil down to the accumulation of all of your days, and will serve as your masterpiece, so be sure to spend time each day chiseling the great sculpture that is your life. Treat each day the same, don't write off days as being "bad, they still count towards the total work of art.

Living a life that feels like a dream is the ultimate goal, isn't it? You don't want to save your best experiences for dreams experienced while you're sleeping, because as tantalizing as they are they aren't real. Having real moment in life that feel surreal and dreamlike is a wonderful thing to have, and the good news is that you can create this with focus and determination by making it your goal. Pick something you think would be a dream to be, do, or have, and then put all of your resources into attaining it. When you get there once you'll be hooked, and you'll want to move onto the next dreamlike moment.

The opposite of this quote is also true, once you give up hope or choose hopelessness, nothing's possible. Hope is the feeling that things will somehow get better, that they will somehow work out. You don't even have to know how it will happen, but it's the believe or even the wish that it will. That's why it's never a good idea to give up hope because you just don't know how things will pan out. When going about your day it's better to feel hopeful about the things you're working on, or the task at hand. If you have hope, it's quite possible that it can all turn out for the best.

It's interesting to think that you can start anew with each passing moment. You can let go of the past, let go of whatever is holding you back, and start again, doing whatever it is you want to do. It's refreshing to know that the present is not entirely enmeshed in the past, and your future is being created moment by moment. If you've been mired in doubt and hesitation to start a new project or to mend a relationship because of things that have happened to you in the past, remember that this moment is totally new and you can move in the direction you want to go.

What a great way to greet the world! Acting might come before believing on this one, as it's not an easy task to believe that it's impossible to fail. It might be a case of faking it until you make it, taking bold actions as if you really believe that you can't fail, and then building up your confidence and your belief that you really can't. Even if things don't work out you still infused them with the right energy, rather than taking a defeatist approach that it probably wouldn't work. It means you'll try bigger and bolder things than if you are doubting yourself the whole time.

It can be dangerous to start counting down your days, because you want to make each one count. But many times there will be an event coming up that makes you start counting down how many days until it arrives. But each day between now and then is important, and you don't want to breeze over any part of your life just to get to the next, seemingly better part. Putting the most of yourself into each day will make it so you never have any regrets about how you spent your time here, and you'll know that you really did make it count each day.

This is a cute way of pointing out the difference between what makes things extraordinary rather than ordinary. It really is a matter of a few degrees, going that little bit further to push things past the point of regularity. The key is that you want to always strive for the extraordinary. Doing a few extraordinary things might make you complacent, and ready to rest on your laurels. But then you run the risk of slipping back into ordinary behaviours. Always ask yourself if what you're doing is ordinary or extraordinary and then give that little extra if needed.

Thoreau points out that it's not enough to get yourself focused in the right direction, but also to give as much effort as possible to propel yourself forward. The situation can arise where you know exactly where you want to go, but you just can't muster up the motivation to build up the momentum to get you there. Another point to consider is that you can spend a lot of energy and give a lot of action, but if you're not pointed in the right direction you won't end up where you want to be. Both are necessary for true success and progress.

Today is your opportunity to make your tomorrow better. If you think of it from the point that your today is the result of your yesterdays, it's clear that what you are doing today is either moving your forward or moving you backward. That's why you want to grab today by the horns and make the most of it as you can. Do that enough times and you'll start to see signs that your todays are getting better, which only sets you up better and better for tomorrow. You can find yourself in negative or positive spiral based on how well you are spending your days.

It's often hard just getting on the right track, but you have to remember that once you're there it's no place to idle. You've got to not only get on the right track, but move yourself forward along that track once you make it there. If it took you a long time to get on the right track, you may find it daunting to have to still give a strong effort to stay on it. But things get easier as you go along, and once you have the hang of it it's easy to stay on the right track and keep the pace so you don't get run over.

The natural instinct is to either get discouraged and give up, or ram up against the roadblock until we knock ourselves out. But what's so bad about taking the long way around as long as you get to your final destination. It does take a bit of belief that the detour is still leading you to where you want to go, and it takes mental fortitude to not get side-tracked along the way and lose sight of where you're going. Once you remove time from the equation and give yourself room to breathe you can actually enjoy taking the scenic route to your goals and dreams.

The power of belief can't be overstated, and it's summed up nicely here. Without belief you'll never get there, so believing that you can is crucial to the process. Believing that you can do it summons the forces of the universe behind you to help you along. Doubting yourself and whether or not you can do it means that you'll only give half-hearted effort, and you won't be nearly as powerful as you could be. Belief can come with time, so don't feel you have to believe you can do it all, just believe that you can accomplish the first step in getting there.

Imagine there's a door marked Fear and behind that door is all of the things you've wished for all of your life. You try to open the door and it's locked. The key is overcoming that fear so that you can have the things you want and be the person you've always wanted to be. Fear is a tricky demon to exorcise. It's different for each of us, and isn't always a very strong feeling. It is sometimes a low-level vibration, that slight underlying feeling of dread that bubbles up when thinking of doing something new or venturing into the unknown.

What things did you start a year ago that you're glad you started back then? If nothing comes to mind, it's high time you start something today that you can be proud of a year from now. If you've already got something in the works, project things out a year from now and imagine how excited you'll be that you already got it going. A year is a long enough time to see some real progress in your efforts, and you are often enjoying the fruits of your labours from a year ago or more. Start something today if you don't have any irons in the fires.

As long as you're alive it's not too late to become the person you really want to be. No matter how bad you might have screwed things up in the past, or no matter how far off course you've gotten from what you really want to do, you can always turn it around. It doesn't take an overhaul in most cases. You can start taking steps towards being what you might have been today. Start implementing little actions into your daily routine to make up for the gap between where you are and where you want to be.

Not many people go the extra mile, which makes it easy for the rest of us to get to where we want to go. They say it's lonely at the top, and this is because few people ever make it that far. Going the extra mile is part of that process, and it's a habit you can start getting into right away if it's not currently a part of your makeup. Try it out on a small scale in your personal relationships, or at your current job. As you make it a habit you'll notice more and more opportunities to go above and beyond, and you'll be able to accomplish more and more.

This is a great way to look around you and see what it is you can do with the resources you have on hand right now. Don't say things like "if only I had this… or "I need to do that before I can do that… as these are just clever ways of putting things off to a future point that never comes. The fact is there are things you could be doing right now that will further your endeavours. Work on those and everything will start to fall in place, you'll be where you need to be, and you'll have what you need to have to get bigger things done.

Struggle often feels like a lack of progress, so it's nice to turn it on its head and realize that it's actually the way progress is made. If you're not struggling you're probably not challenging yourself enough. The important part is not to let struggle deter you from making that progress. Step one is learning to view struggling as a positive thing, rather than a negative thing. Then you won't be so hard on yourself if you find that you're struggling again. It just means you're learning, growing, and taking on enough to keep you busy.

To become a great leader and staying positive requires a stress free mind. I think I say this with an obvious approach that a stress free mind at all times, may be impossible. It all comes down to being mind-full, mind-full of all your emotions and surroundings. Mindfulness is literally being aware, calming one self and soaking in the beauty of each species and our beautiful planet. Being mind-full of all emotions in the mind and body, but not always acting upon them.

The beauty of our world can be us.

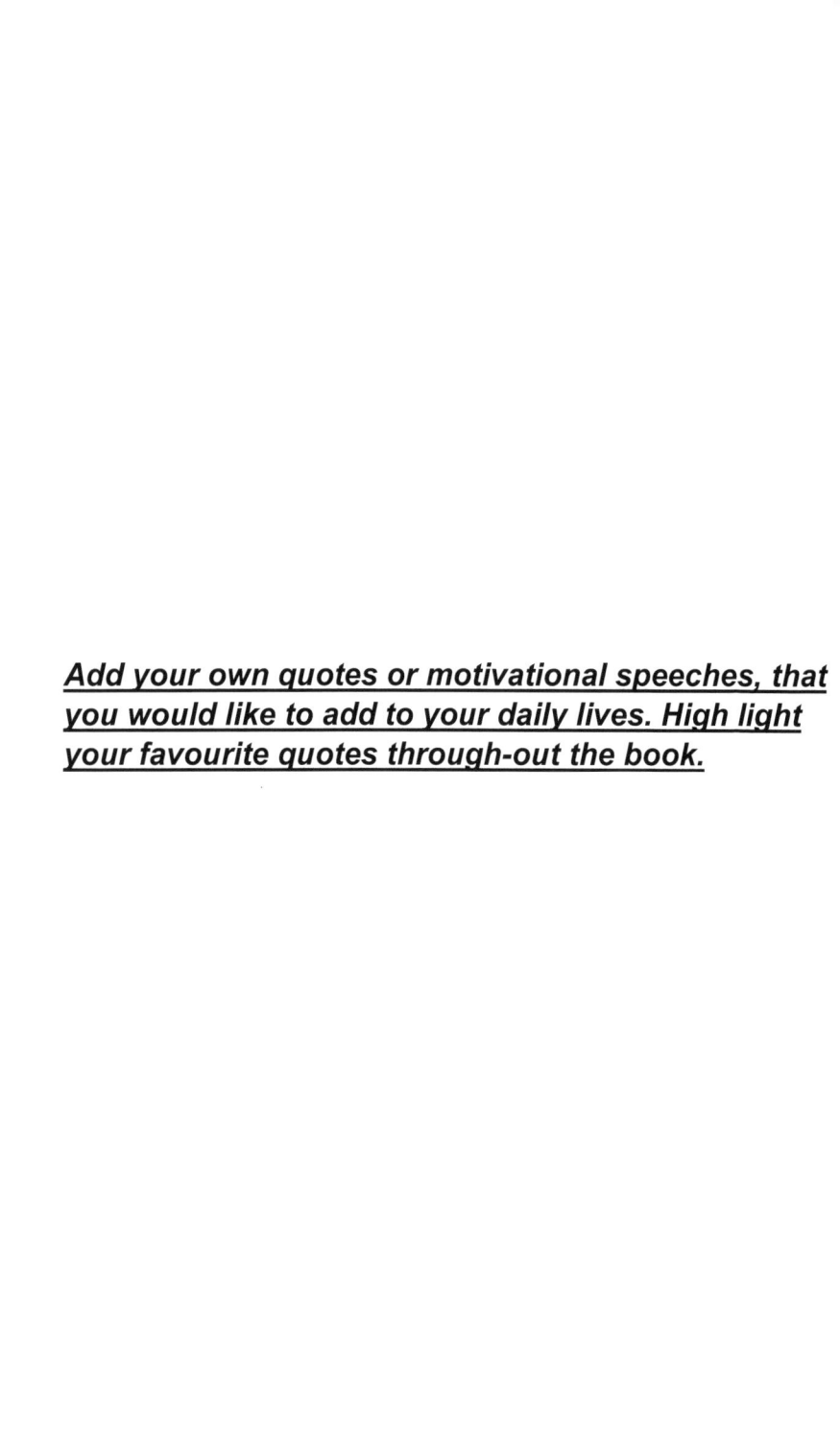

Add your own quotes or motivational speeches, that you would like to add to your daily lives. High light your favourite quotes through-out the book.

Write down your goals below.

One month. (short-term)

First goal: (try and write time and date by each goal, also date you would like to achieve by, this is your deadline, no-body else's, nobody is forcing you, this is all of your own dreams and wishes. You have got this. Also make as many goals as you want, no matter how small or big. It could be something as simple as I will wash my work mug every day for a month. Anything you want or feel like you need to achieve)

Time:

Date:

Date wanting to achieve by:

Date achieved by:

Second goal:

Time:

Date:

Date wanting to achieve by:

Date achieved by:

Third goal:

Time:

Date:

Date wanting to achieve by:

Date achieved by:

Fourth goal:

Time:

Date:

Date wanting to achieve by:

Date achieved by:

Two months

First goal:

Time:

Date:

Date to achieve by:

Date achieved by:

Three months

First goal:

Time:

Date:

Date to achieve by:

Date achieved by:

How did I feel:

Six months (mid-term)

One year

Two years

Five years

Ten years (long-term)

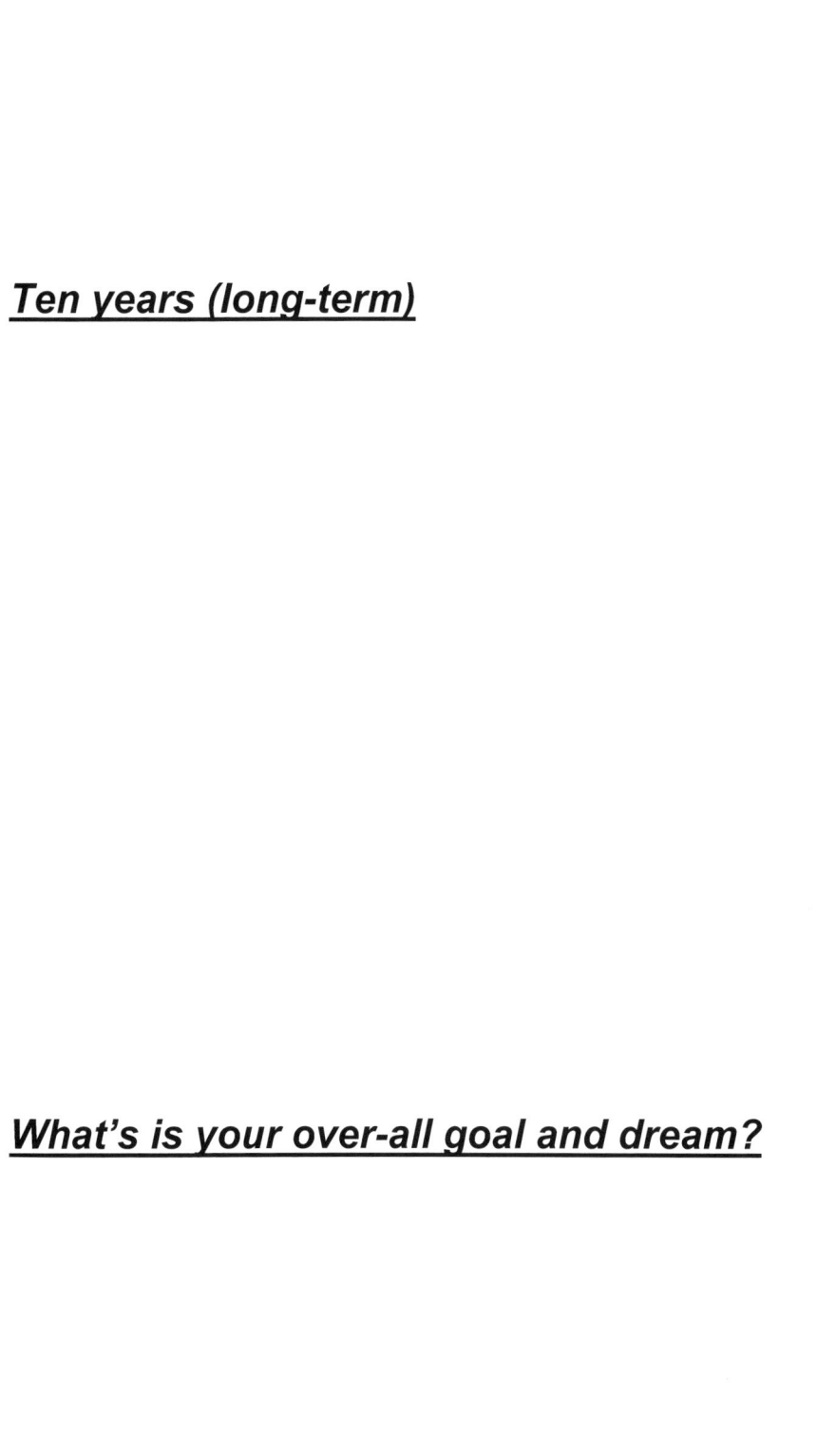

What's is your over-all goal and dream?

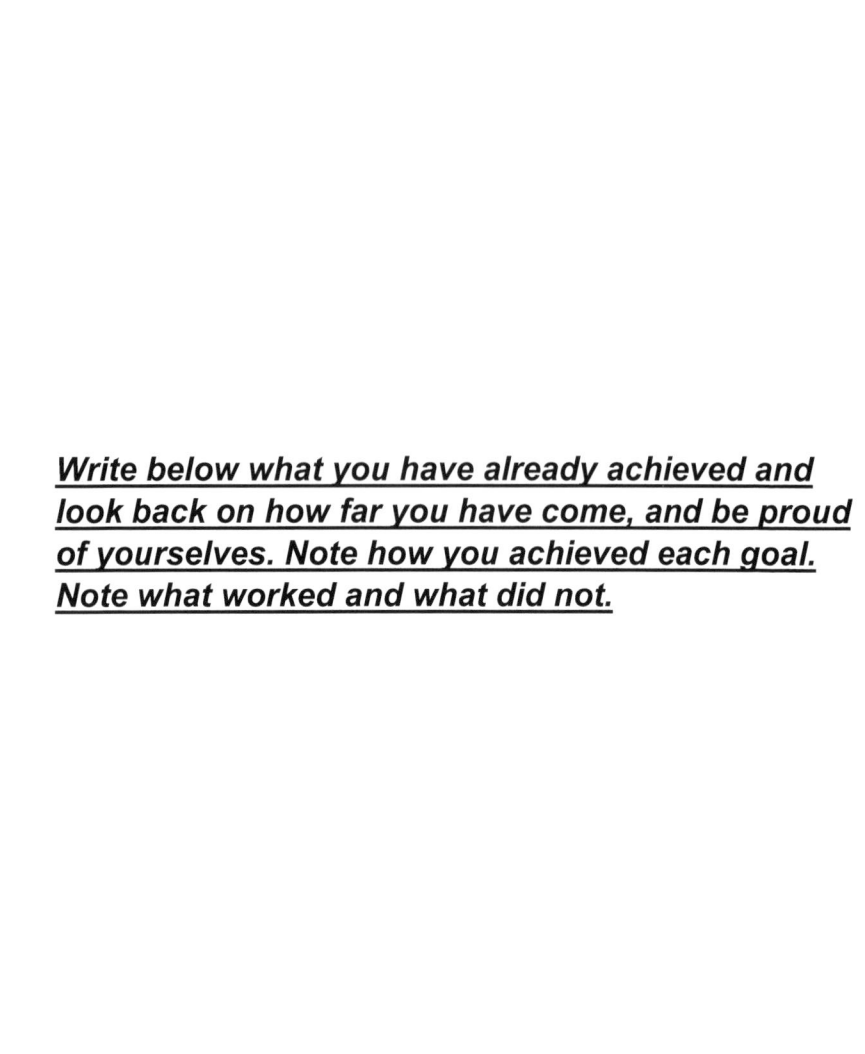

Write below what you have already achieved and look back on how far you have come, and be proud of yourselves. Note how you achieved each goal. Note what worked and what did not.

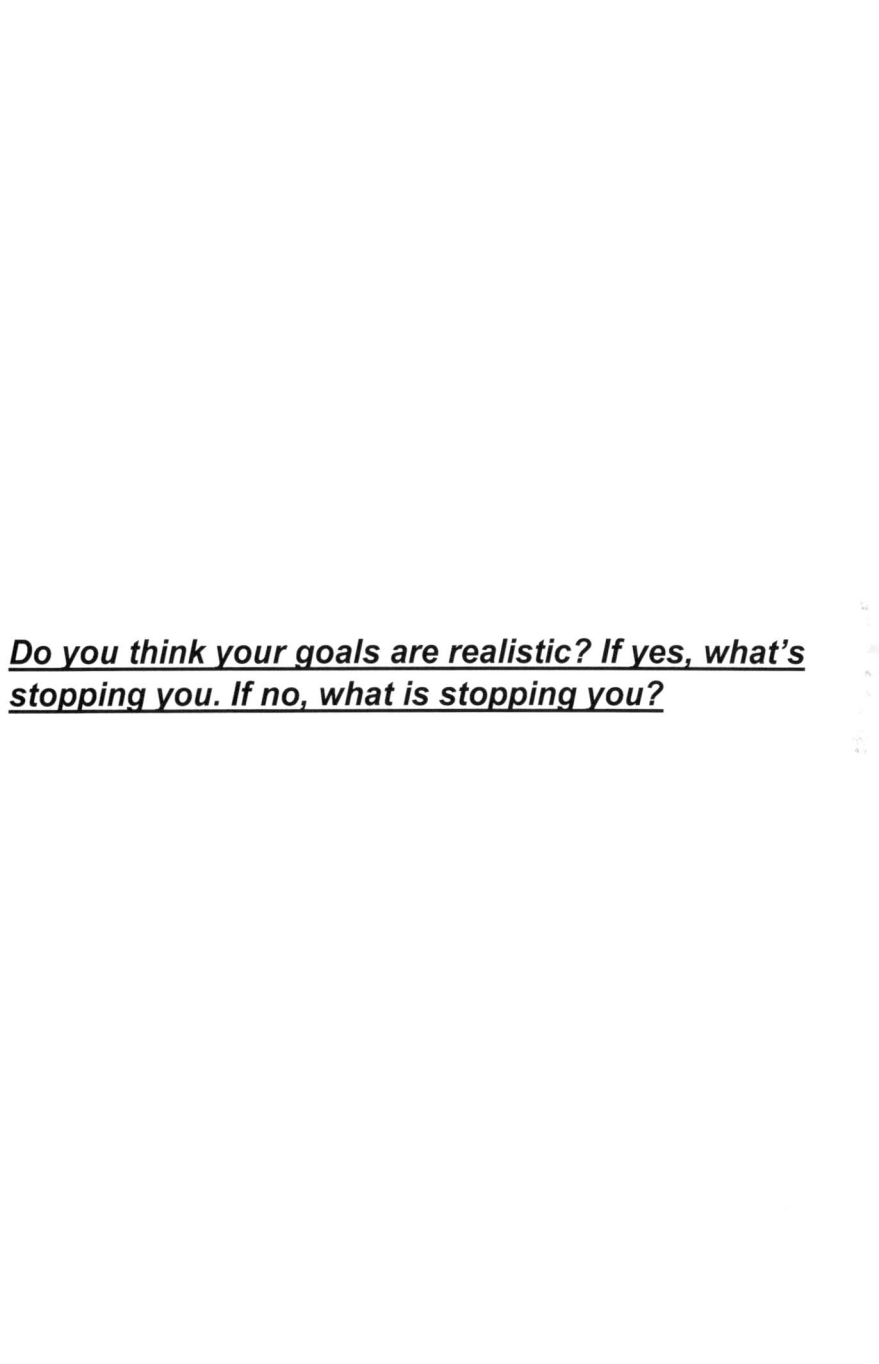

Do you think your goals are realistic? If yes, what's stopping you. If no, what is stopping you?

A goal can be a long process and sometimes obstacles will get in the way. Obstacles can be fun, enjoy them, enjoy learning. You aim/goal can still be achieved.

Managers you can use these guide lines with your staff- what is their short term (one-month goal) and what is their long term (one year or more goal). You as the manager can help them gain clarity and guide them.

This goal process can also be used for home life. For e.g. woman wanting to fall pregnant, one-month goal…. I will work out my most fertile time of the month, or at least start that process and eat the correct fertile aiding food. Long term goal…. Fall pregnant, have the most stunning child ever seen. Men you can use this at home, gym etc. short term goal for e.g. purchase protein, measure width, lifting 50kg. long term goal. width doubled and lifting double. (yes, I don't understand each subject entirely, but this is just for an example)

Parents, you can also use this for your children. E.g. one-month goal... parents class or behaviour charts…. Six-month goal. behaved well, trip to Lego land earned or that toy he/she has been beginning for. For older children doing exams… one- month goal, study nights Monday to Wednesday 5-7 pm. Six months for doing their study, they earn the trainers they were after or they have passed an exam etc.

The goal stages could be used for saving and finance gain. One-month goal. I will sort through my belongings and see what I can sell? Two-month goal, car boot. Six-month goal, I have cut out buying an extra drink at the shop each day and sweets etc. I have saved 40 pounds a week and in one month I have saved 160 pounds from doing this… (yes, I know you're thinking, wow 40 pounds on rubbish, an extreme example for some, but true for other's) one-year goal, I have now saved up 2000 for our family holiday or 20,000 for a deposit on a house. Etc….

This goal scale can be used in any way; you feel you need to achieve anything you want. As long as you make each stage, realistic to you. Than you should achieve your own goal.

Remember to re-check your goals. Adjust if you need to. Time and date each goal you have set. Make them smaller so they are more achievable. When you feel dis-heartened or struggle, read through the quotes. Imagine yourself at the final goal and how happy you feel, being in that position of your final goal complete. Than go back and re-asses your goals and follow your dreams.

I will leave the last few pages empty: take notes, write whatever you need too. This is your book. Do what you need to do, to achieve your goal and love and peace.

How do you feel? About achieving each Goal?

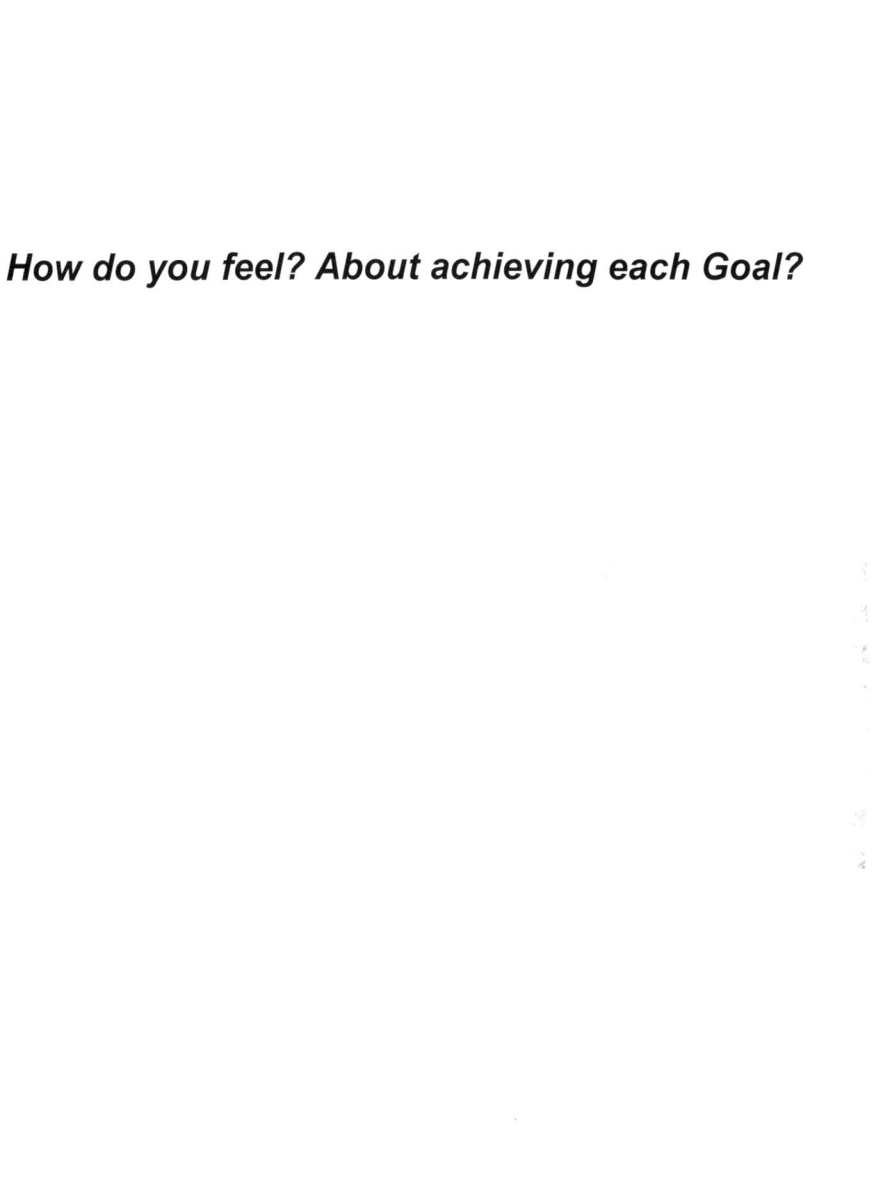

What are your strengths? In life and work?

What are your weaknesses? In life and work?

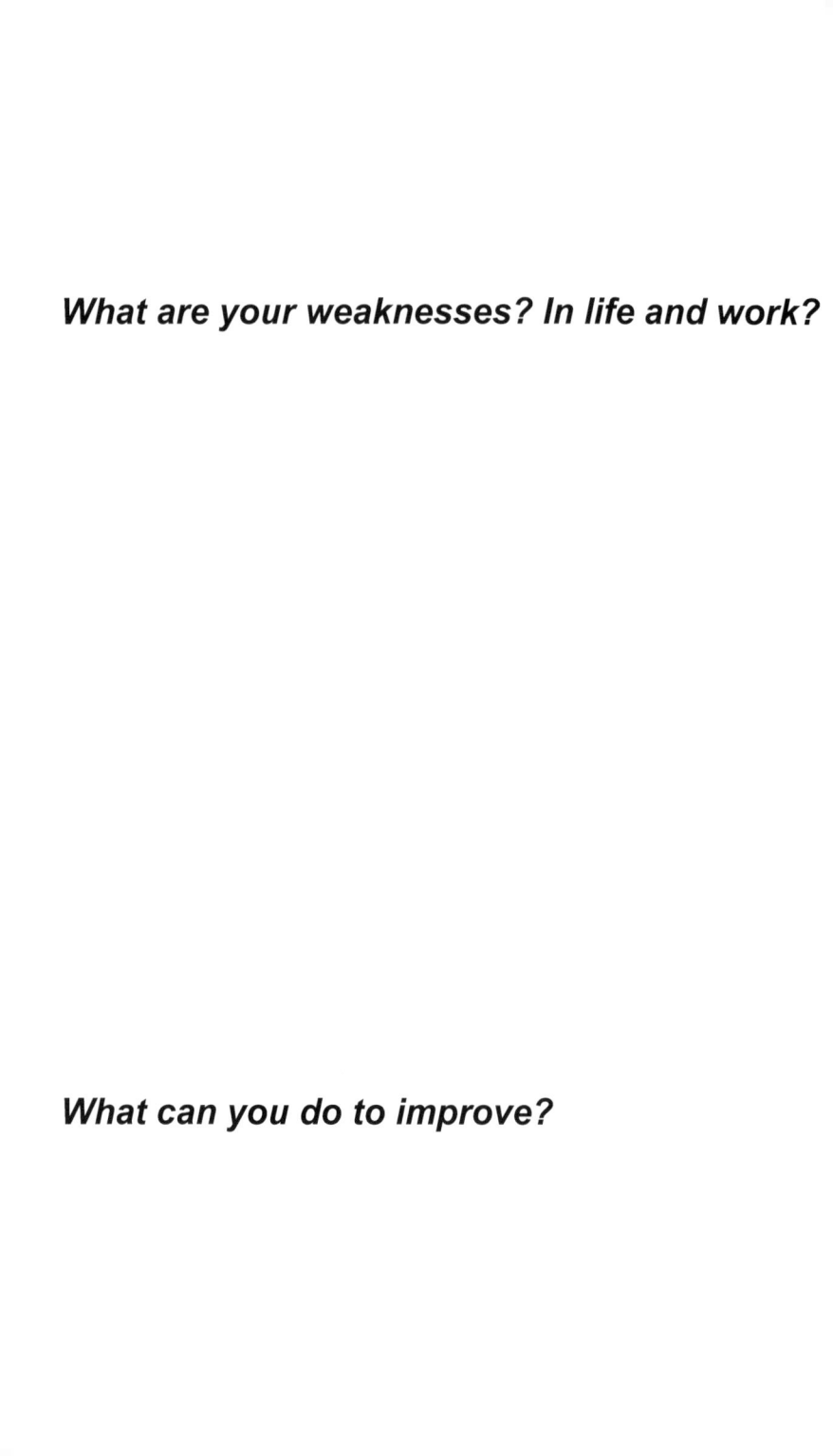

What can you do to improve?

Who are you doing all this for?

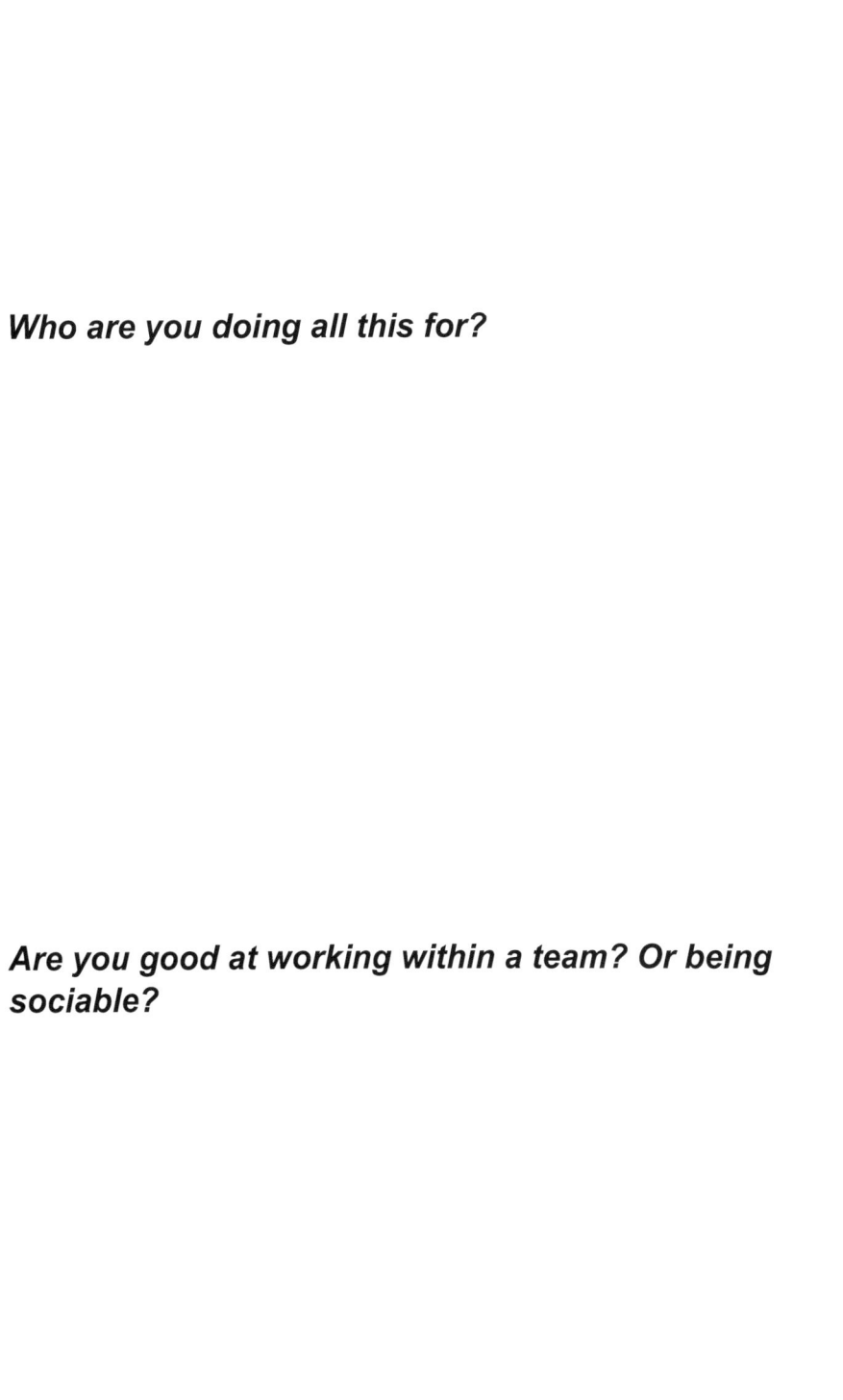

Are you good at working within a team? Or being sociable?

Are you good at working as an individual? Or being in solitude?

Are your kind enough to other human beings and animals?

Do you eat the correct food for your body?

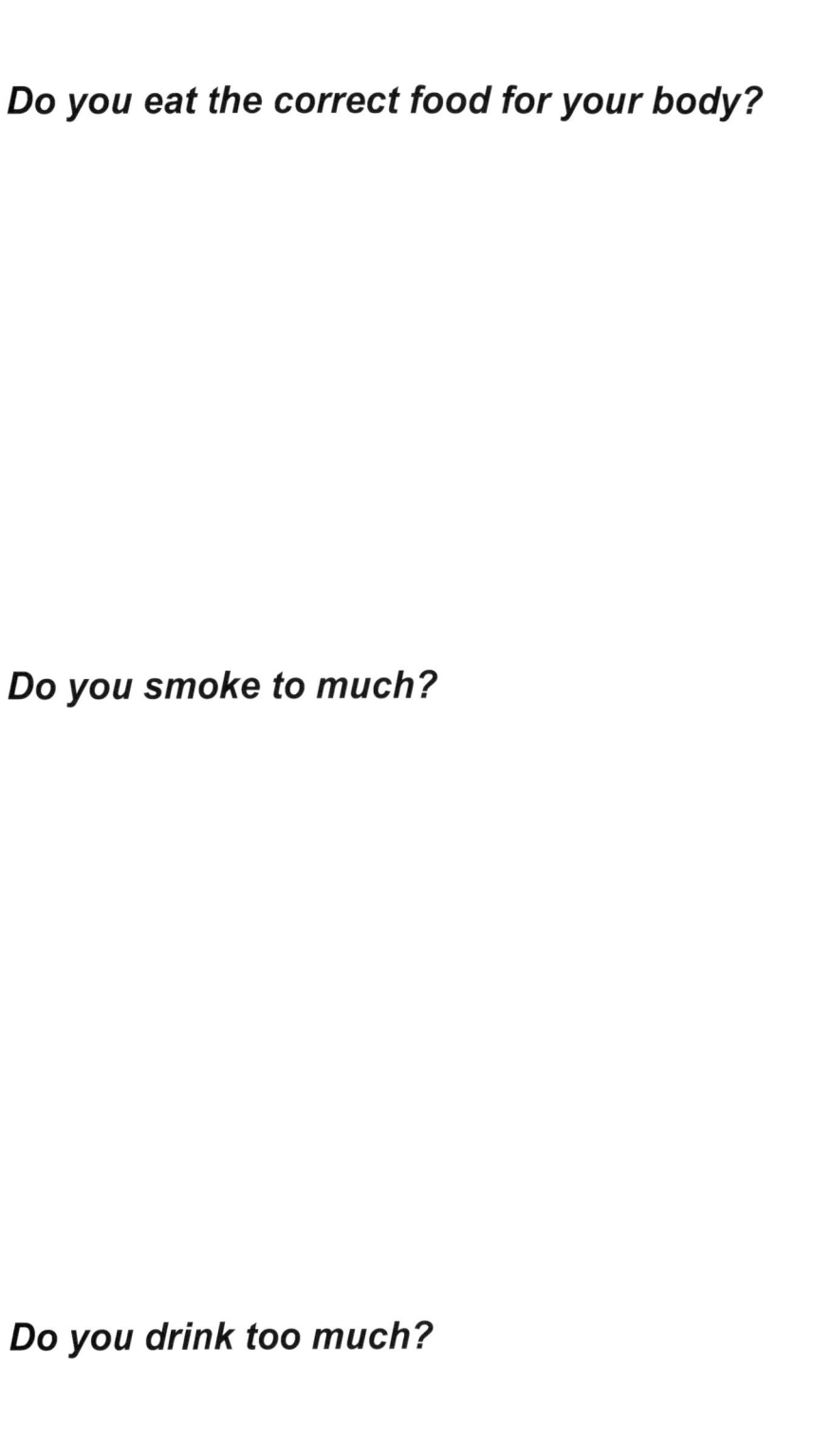

Do you smoke to much?

Do you drink too much?

Do you exercise to much or not enough?

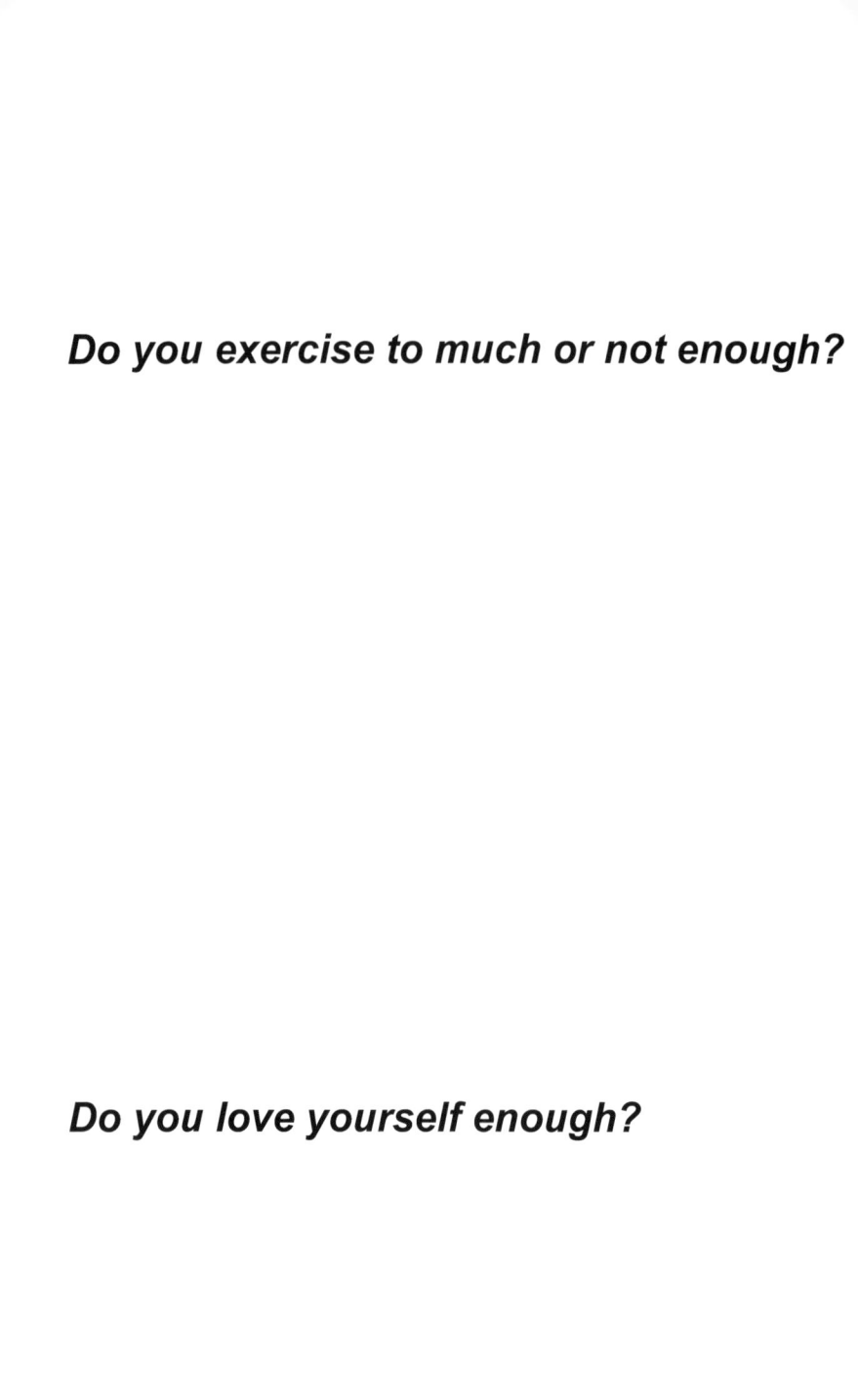

Do you love yourself enough?

Can you be a better person?

If you answer yes, you know what to do. Set goals and achieve them. If you answer No, then I have no words you are an awesome human being. But so are you who said yes, you were honest with yourself. Nobody else is reading the book in your hands, its personal to you, and only you. I should most definitely love myself more. I can definitely be a better person. I always want to improve myself. What's living if we never want to improve or do something new. This is what life is about improving ourselves and others around us.

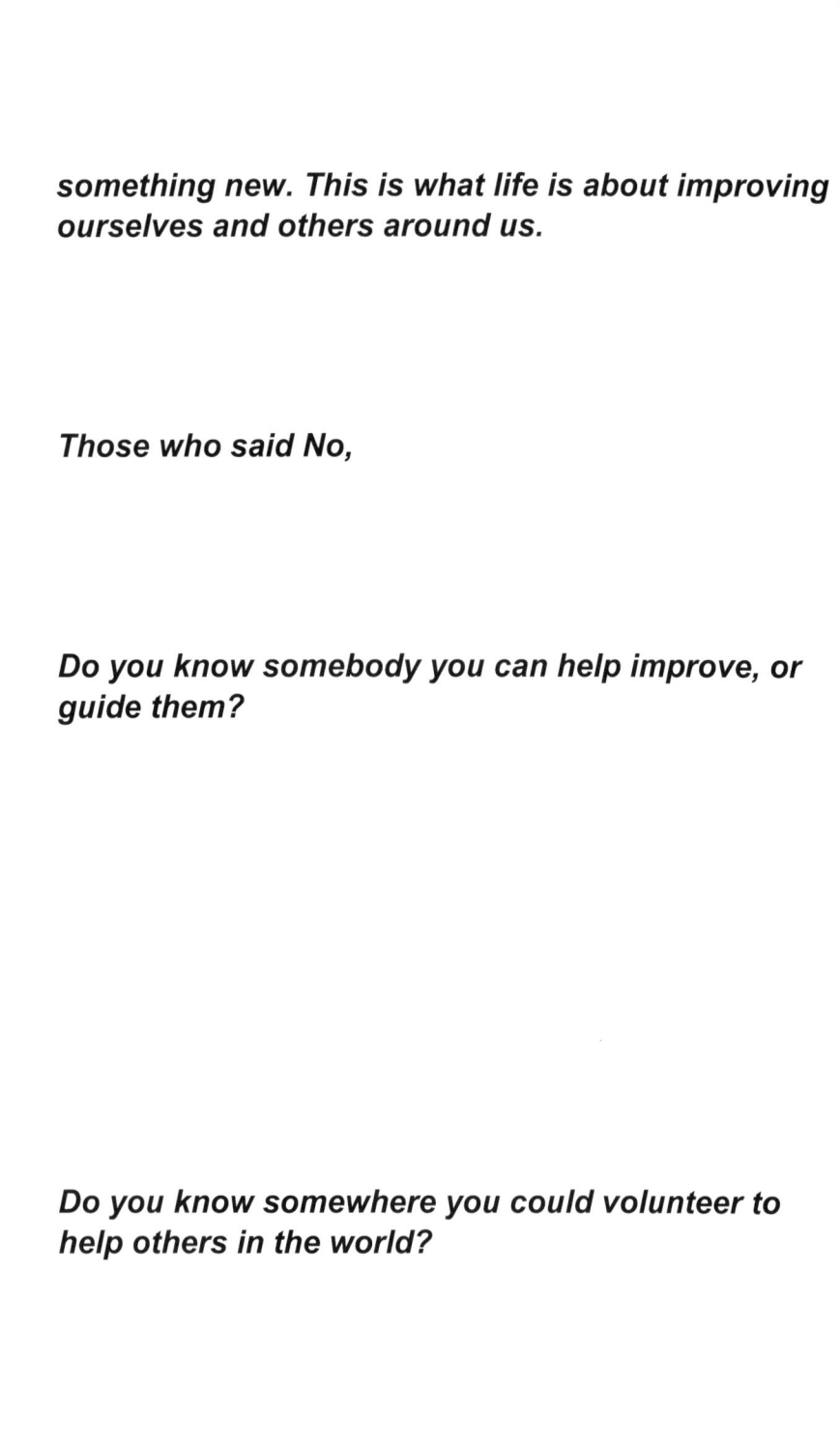

Those who said No,

Do you know somebody you can help improve, or guide them?

Do you know somewhere you could volunteer to help others in the world?

Do you know somebody you can pass you knowledge too, help strengthen another?

How?

Where?

When?

I love you all, we are all amazing people. Let's all start helping ourselves and others to follow dreams. Dreams that will turn into reality.

Find your motivational quote, your motivational hero. Get a paper copy of your quote or image and stick it on your fridge. Remind yourself every single day of this motivation. It could be you in ten years' time, whatever it is, use it. Let it motivate you, to your highest self.

Motivate you.

Motivate your friend or foe.

Inspire yourself.

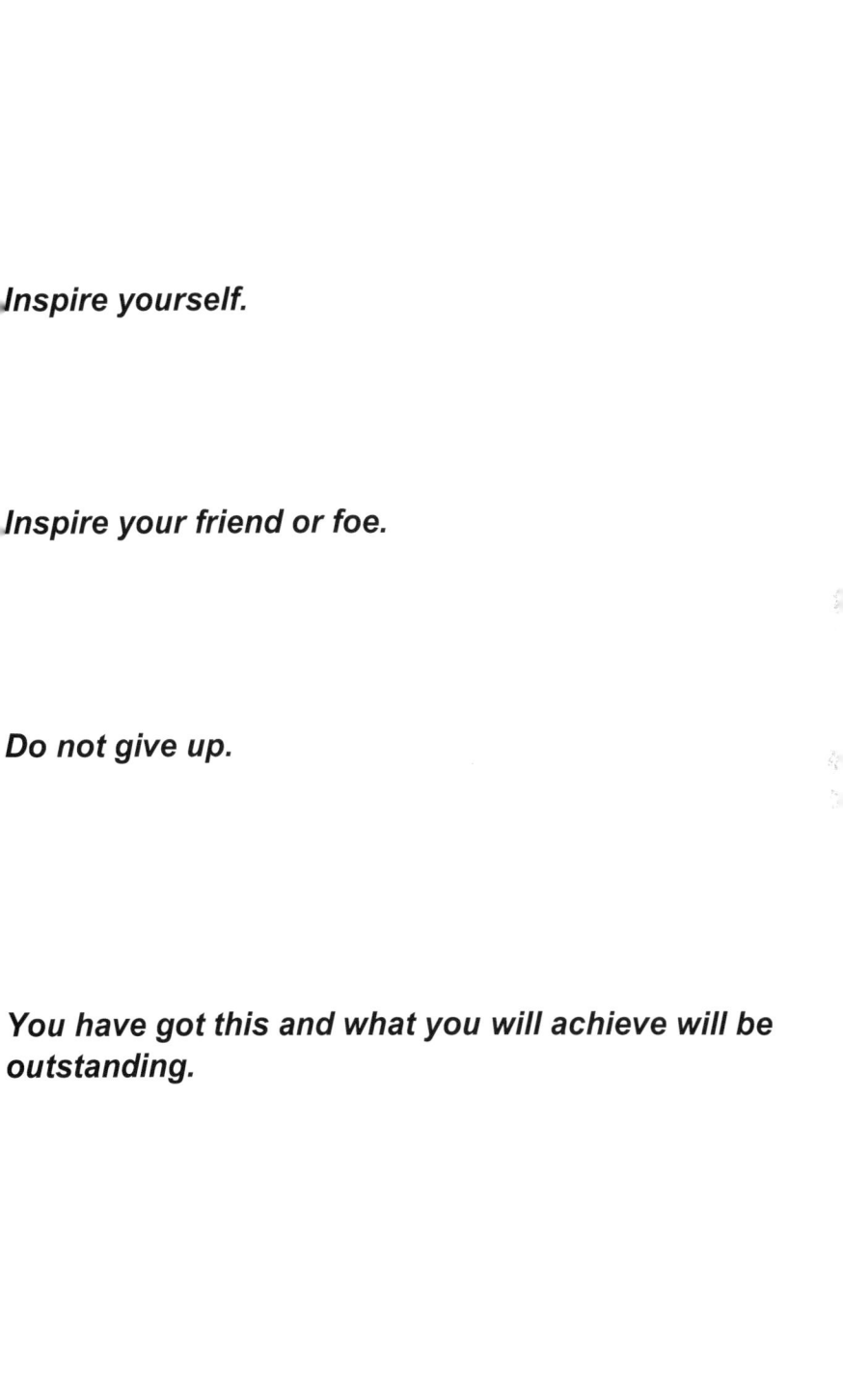

Inspire your friend or foe.

Do not give up.

You have got this and what you will achieve will be outstanding.

Printed in Great Britain
by Amazon